SURVEY OF ENGLISH LITERATURE AND CULTURE

edited by

Hartmut Ilsemann

Bibliografische Informationen der Deutschen Nationalbibliothek:

Die Deutsche Nationalbibliothek verzeichnet diese Publikation in der Deutschen Nationalbibliografie; detaillierte bibliografische Daten sind im Internet über http://dnb.dnb.de abzurufen.

Herstellung und Verlag:

BoD – Books on Demand, Norderstedt

ISBN: 978-3-7534-4304-1

The original version of this survey of English literary and cultural history consisted of individual A4 sheets, each covering twenty years. At the top of the page the English rulers were named, below them the Scottish kings. This was followed by data on history and, at the bottom of the page, data on people who played a role in politics, literature, music and culture. In this way, five sheets provided information about one century. The dates 1000 AD to 2000 AD resulted in a total of fifty sheets, which for years have divided epochs and periods in the corridor of the English Department of the Leibniz University of Hanover and sometimes offered a final orientation shortly before exams.

The overview was prepared by students in a cultural studies seminar when computers and word processing had become available for the first time. Sources were largely omitted due to the overview character and lack of space, normally indispensable in academic papers. Only later additions are based on specific sources. If these have not been named, they are taken from the English Wikipedia.

In the present version, three pages have been added with information on the settlement of England, the Old English period and Christianisation, as well as two sheets on the period from 2000 to 2020. [1]

---

[1] The term "English" is first and foremost language-related, but much of the information applies to the whole of Britain

The Settlement of Britain

The earliest evidence for early modern humans in North West Europe is a jawbone discovered in Devon at Kents Cavern in 1927, between 41,000 und 44,000 years old. The region has numerous remains from the Mesolithic, Neolithic and Bronze Age, such as **Stonehenge and Avebury**.

Stonehenge

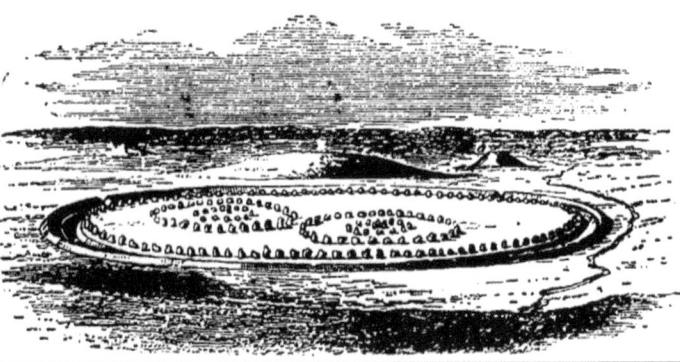
Avebury

In the Iron Age all Britain was inhabited by the Celtic people known as Britons, including Belgic tribes. In 43 AD the Roman Conquest of Britain began. They maintained control of their province of Britannia until the early 5th century.

The end of Roman rule brought the Anglo-Saxon settlement of Britain, various Germanic people established several kingdoms. According to early sources, **Hengist and Horsa** arrived in Britain at Ebbsfleet on the Isle of Thanet. For a time they served as mercenaries for **Vortigern**, King of the Britons, but later they turned against him. Horsa was killed in fighting the Britons, but Hengist successfully conquered Kent, become the forefather of its kings.

Old English replaced the previous British language whose speakers retreated to Cornwall and Wales. Raids by Vikings became frequent after 800 AD, and the Norsemen settled in large parts of England. When the various Anglo-Saxon kingdoms united the Kingdom of England came into being by the 10th century.

Christianisation

St. Martins Church at Canterbury.

The most powerful ruler in England was Æthelbert of Kent who married a Frankish princess, Bertha of Paris as there were strong trade connections between Kent and the Franks. The marriage was agreed to on the condition that she be allowed to practice her religion. St. Martin's church, just outside the city Walls of Canterbury, was the private chapel of Queen Bertha who died in 1601 or just after. In 1595 Pope Gregory had sent Augustine to Canterbury to head the mission, he arrived on the Isle of Thanet in **1597** and established his base at Canterbury. After Augustine's death in 604, the monastery SS. Peter and Paul was named for him and eventually became a missionary school.

Many of the first churches, well before 1597 after Constantine had allowed the Christian faith in his empire, were built on or in former pagan places of worship, such as prominent hilltops or groves, as these places were already considered sacred and those who were to be missionaries continued to gather there. St. Patrick had christianised Ireland in the 5th century and Columban started his mission in Scotland, and then moved south to Northumberland. The two missions clashed. But the **Synod of Whitby in 664** decided in favour of the Roman rite. Numerous missionaries also travelled from England to the continent, devoting themselves in particular to the Germanic peoples who are related to the Anglo-Saxons. *In his Historia ecclesiastica gentis Anglorum*, the principle source for the Synod, **Bede** declared that after Whitby, 'all present … gave up their imperfect rules'.

Old English – the earliest form of the English language – was spoken and written in Anglo-Saxon Britain from c. 450 CE until c. 1150 (thus it continued to be used for some decades after the Norman Conquest of 1066). According to Toronto University's Dictionary of Old English Corpus, the entire surviving body of Old English material from 600 to 1150 consists of only 3,037 texts (excluding manuscripts with minor variants), amounting to a mere three million words. A single prolific modern author easily exceeds this total: Charles Dickens's fiction, for example, amounts to over four million words. While three million words is not a great deal of data for a period in linguistic history extending over five centuries, it is enough to allow us to make a confident description of the linguistic character of Old English and to plot its evolution into Middle English. The development is most evident in vocabulary and grammar.

Danelaw can describe the set of legal terms and definitions created in the treaties between **Alred the Great**, the king of Wessex, and **Guthrum**, the Danish warlord, written following Guthrum's defeat at the Battle of Edington in 878.

In 886, the Treaty of Alfred and Guthrum was formalised, defining the boundaries of their kingdoms, with provisions for peaceful relations between the English and the Vikings. The language spoken in England was affected by this clash of cultures, with the emergence of Anglo-Norse dialects.

800 – Waves of Danish assaults on the coastlines of the British Isles.

848/9	Alfred the Great	899

850 852 854 856 858 860 862 864 866 868 870 872 874 876 878 880 882 884 886 888 890 892 894 896 898 900

King of Wessex 871   –   886

King of the Anglo-Saxons 886   –   ✝ 26 October 899

865 – Danish raiders first begin to settle in England. Led by the brothers Halfdan and Ivar the Boneless, they wintered in East Anglia, where they demanded and received tribute in exchange for a temporary peace. From there, they move north and attack Northumbria, which is in the midst of a civil war between the deposed king Osberht and a usurper Ælla. The Danes use the civil turmoil as an opportunity to capture York, which they sack and burn.

867 – Following the loss of York, Osberht and Ælla form an alliance against the Danes. They launch a counter-attack, but the Danes kill both Osberht and Ælla and set up a puppet king on the Northumbrian throne. In response, King Æthelred of Wessex, along with his brother Alfred, march against the Danes, who are positioned behind fortifications in Nottingham, but are unable to draw them into battle. In order to effect peace, King Burgred of Mercia cedes Nottingham to the Danes in exchange for leaving the rest of Mercia undisturbed. **868** – Danes capture Nottingham.

BRITISH ISLES
about 886
(at the time of Danish conquest)

The Danelaw - conquests of the Danes

Anglo-saxon states

Lands of the Britons

The Five Danish fortified "boroughs"
R. Botev, 2006

869 – Ivar the Boneless returns and demands tribute from King Edmund of East Anglia.

870 – King Edmund refuses Ivar's demand. Ivar defeats and captures Edmund at Hoxne, adding East Anglia to the area controlled by the invading Danes. King Æthelred and Alfred attack the Danes at Reading, but are repulsed with heavy losses. The Danes pursue them.

871 – On 7 January, Æthelred and Alfred make their stand at Ashdown (on what is the Berkshire/North Wessex Downs now in Oxfordshire). Æthelred could not be found at the start of battle, as he was busy praying in his tent, so Alfred leads the army into battle. Æthelred and Alfred defeat the Danes, who count among their losses five jarls (nobles). The Danes retreat and set up fortifications at Basingstoke in Hampshire, a mere 14 miles (23 km) from Reading. Æthelred attacks the Danish fortifications and is routed. The Danes follow up with another victory in March at Meretum (now Marton, Wiltshire).

871 23 April ✝ King Æthelred dies and Alfred takes the throne of Wessex. For the rest of the year Alfred concentrates on attacking with small bands against isolated groups of Danes. He is moderately successful in this endeavour and is able to score minor victories against the Danes, but his army is on the verge of collapse. Alfred responds by paying off the Danes in order for a promise of peace. During the peace, the Danes turn north and attack Mercia, which they finish off in short order, and capture London in the process. King Burgred of Mercia fights in vain against Ivar the Boneless and his Danish invaders for three years until 874, when he flees to Europe. During Ivar's campaign against Mercia he dies and is succeeded by Guthrum the Old. Guthrum quickly defeats Burgred and places a puppet on the throne of Mercia. The Danes now control East Anglia, Northumbria and Mercia, with only Wessex continuing to resist.

875 – The Danes settle in Dorset, well inside of Alfred's Kingdom of Wessex, but Alfred quickly makes peace

The Exeter Book, which belongs to the Dean and Chapter of Exeter Cathedral, is one of the four most significant verse manuscripts to survive from the Anglo-Saxon period. These four books contain the vast majority of all surviving Old English poetry. Almost all of the texts in these manuscripts are unique, and so without them we would have a much poorer understanding of the earliest period in English literature. The Exeter Book was made in c. 960–80. It was copied by one scribe from a variety of exemplars (textual sources). In the 11th century it seems to have been acquired for Exeter Cathedral by Bishop Leofric (died 1072). A list of donations left by Leofric to the Cathedral, dated to 1069–72, mentions 'mycel Englisc boc be gehwilcum þingum on leoðwisum geworht' ['a large English book about many things written in verse']. In all likelihood, this refers to the Exeter Book.

876 – The Danes break the peace when they capture the fortress of followed by a similar capture of Exeter in 877.

877 – Alfred lays in a siege, while the Danes wait for reinforcements from Scandinavia. Unfortunately for the Danes, the fleet of reinforcements encounter a storm and lose more than 100 ships, and the Danes are forced to return to East Mercia in the north.

878 – In January, Guthrum leads an attack against Wessex that seeks to capture Alfred while he winters in Chippenham. Another Danish army landed in south Wales arrives and moves south with the intent of intercepting Alfred should he flee from Guthrum's forces. However, they stop during their march to capture a small fortress at Countisbury Hill, held by a Wessex ealdorman named Odda. The Saxons, led by Odda, attack the Danes while they sleep and defeat their superior forces, saving Alfred from being trapped between the two armies. Alfred is forced to go into hiding for the rest of the winter and spring of 878 in the Somerset marshes in order to avoid the superior Danish forces. In the spring, Alfred is able to gather an army and attacks Guthrum and the Danes at Edington. The Danes are defeated and retreat to Chippenham, where the English pursue and lay siege to Guthrum's forces. The Danes are unable to hold out without relief and soon surrender. Alfred demands as a term of the surrender that Guthrum become baptised as a Christian, which Guthrum agrees to do, with Alfred acting as his godfather. Guthrum is true to his word and settles in East Anglia, at least for a while.

884 – Guthrum attacks Kent, but is defeated by the English. This leads to the Treaty of Alfred and Guthrum, which establishes the boundaries of the Danelaw.

900   1000

| 900 | 905 | 910 | 915 | 920 | 925 | 930 | 935 | 940 | 945 | 950 | 955 | 960 | 970 | 975 | 980 | 985 | 990 | 995 | 1000 |

902 – Essex submits to Æthelwald.

903 – Æthelwald incites the East Anglian Danes into breaking the peace. They ravage Mercia before winning a pyrrhic victory that saw the death of Æthelwald and the Danish King Eohric; this allows Edward the Elder to consolidate power.

911 – The English defeat the Danes at the Battle of Tettenhall. The Northumbrians ravage Mercia but are trapped by Edward and forced to fight.

917 – In return for peace and protection, the Kingdoms of Essex and East Anglia accept Edward the Elder as their suzerain overlord. Æthelflæd, Lady of the Mercians, takes the borough of Derby.

918 – The borough of Leicester submits peaceably to Æthelflæd's rule. The people of York promise to accept her as their overlord, but she dies before this could come to fruition. She is succeeded by her brother, the Kingdoms of Mercia and Wessex united in the person of King Edward.

919 – Norwegian Vikings under King Ragnvald Sygtryggsson of Dublin take York.

920 – Edward is accepted as father and lord by the King of the Scots, by Rægnold, the sons of Eadulf, the English, Norwegians, Danes and others all of whom dwell in Northumbria and the King and people of the Strathclyde Welsh.   954 – King Eric is driven out of Northumbria, his death marking the end of the prospect of a Northern Viking Kingdom stretching from York to Dublin and the Isles.

1002 - St. Brice's Day massacre of the Danes

1066 – **Harald Hardrada** lands with an army, hoping to take control of York and the English crown. He is defeated and killed at the Battle of Stamford Bridge. This event is often cited as the end of the Viking era. The same year, William the Conqueror, himself a descendant of Vikings, successfully took the English throne and became the first Norman king of England.

1069 – **Sweyn II** of Denmark lands with an army, in much the same way as Harald Hardrada. He took control of York after defeating the Norman garrison and inciting a local uprising. King William eventually defeated his forces and devastated the region in the Harrying of the North.

1075 – One of Sweyn's sons, **Knut**, set sail for England to support an English rebellion, but it had been crushed before he arrived, so he settled for plundering the city of York and surrounding area, before returning home.

1085 – **Knut**, now king, planned a major invasion against England but the assembled fleet never sailed. Other than Eystein II of Norway taking advantage of the civil war during Stephen's reign, to plunder the east coast of England,[22] there were no serious invasions or raids of England by the Danes after this.

The **Anglo-Saxon Chronicle** is a collection of annals in Old English chronicling the history of the Anglo-Saxons. The original manuscript of the Chronicle was created late in the 9th century, probably in Wessex, during the reign of **Alfred the Great** (r. 871–899). Multiple copies were made of that one original and then distributed to monasteries across England, where they were independently updated. In one case, the Chronicle was still being actively updated in 1154.

he Junius manuscript, also known as the Cædmon manuscript, is an illustrated collection of poems on biblical narratives.

The **Vercelli Book** contains both poetry and prose; it is not known how it came to be in Vercelli.

The **Beowulf** Manuscript (British Library Cotton Vitellius A. xv), sometimes called the Nowell Codex, contains prose and poetry, typically dealing with monstrous themes, including Beowulf.

1000	Ethelred	1013	Swein	1014	Ethelred		1016	Canute			1020

1000	1001	1002	1003	1004	1005	1006	1007	1008	1009	1010	1011	1012	1013	1014	1015	1016	1017	1018	1019	1020

1000 Kenneth III	1005	Malcolm II	1020

Viking ship in early manuscript

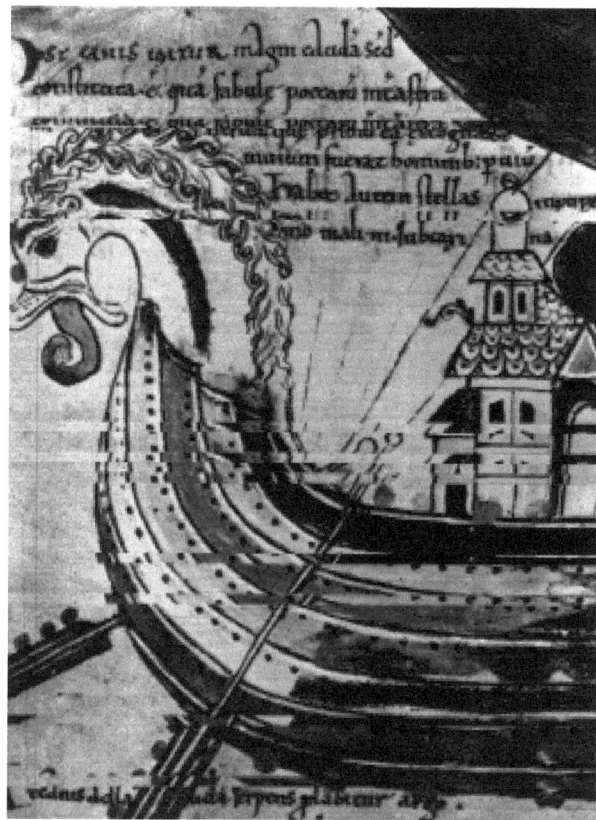

1012 Vikings (under Swein of Denmark) plunder Canterbury Cathedral and murder the Archbishop

1013 Swein decides to conquer all of England; is accepted as English king in autumn; Ethelred flees to Normandy

Swein ✝ **1014** Ethelred is recalled

Ethelred ✝ **April 1014** dies in London

1016 Struggle between Ethelred's son Edmund, whom the citizens of London and the noble men wanted as king and Canute of Denmark, Swein's son, whom the clerus and influential people wanted

November 1016

Edmund ✝, assassinated by a follower of Canute. Canute rules with a policy uniting the Danish and the English part of Britain's population

Canute summons leading Danes and Englishmen to Oxford **1018**, they promise to live peacefully together under the "Laws of Edgar" (Edgar the Peaceable 959 - 975)

Canute becomes King of Denmark **1019**

1014 Wulfstan:"*Sermo Lupi ad Anglos*" (Address to the English)

Aelfric ✝ **1010**

1002 Wulfstan becomes Archbishop of York and Bishop of Worcester

1005 Aelfric becomes Abbot of Eynsham

Old English Literature (before 1066)

Main forms of poetry were
- sagas and fairy tales
- elegies
- religious poetry

Main forms of prose were homilies, sermons and moralizing texts, which were read in church at appointed times of the ecclesiastical year. Apart from this, prose was mainly a translation of biblical or philosophical texts.

Outstanding authors of the early 11th century:

Aelfric
(*955 ✝1010)
- Monk in Winchester, Cerne Abbas
- Abbot of Eynsham from 1005   -
- Wrote in Old English idiom in an age when everybody else used Latin -

Main Works:
Catholic Homilies **(2 vol.) 990-992**
Live of Saints **992-998**
Translations (e.g. *Heptateuch*, *Interrogationes Sigewulfii*)
First Latin Grammar ("Grammar") in Old English as well as *"Colloquy"*, a dialogue between teacher and student

Wulfstan
(✝ 1023)
Bishop of London (996) and Worcester (1002)
Archbishop of York (1002)
(held sees of Worcester and York simultaneously)
drafted codes of law for both, Ethelred (from 1008- 1015) and for Canute (from 1016-1023)

Main Works:
several English homilies (even though only four homilies and one pastoral letter can be ascribed to him with some probability)
"Sermo Lupi ad Anglos" **1014**
(= Address to the English)

Four very important manuscripts of Old English Literature were written around the turn of the millennium. All of them were collections of poetry:
"Junius-Manuscript", "Exeter-Book", "Vercelli-Book", "Beowulf-Manuscript"
Beowulf-Manuscript:
Even though the saga of Beowulf had been heard of as early as the 8th century, it was only written down around 1000. The poem contains 3182 lines and tells of two events in the life of the hero: Beowulf. It contains many Christian and historic allusions, even though they contradict each other. The historical events put the story into the 6th century, a time when the Christianisation of Britain had just started. Beowulf is seen as the first major poem in a European language and it is definitely the most important Old English poem.

Early Scholasticism:

School of philosophical systems and speculative tendencies of various medieval Christian thinkers from the 9th to the 12th century (especially Anselm of Canterbury, 1033-1109, archbishop of Canterbury from 1093 - 1109). They were working on a background of fixed religious dogma, trying to solve general philosophical problems of faith and reason, will and intellect, realism (character of being) and nominalism (character of names) and prove the existence of God.

In those days Aristotle's influence on "modern" philosophy grew as the nature of knowledge was discussed. The most important philosopher of that time was Peter Abelard (1079-1142) who pitched the moderate realism of the Aristotelians against the extreme realism of the Platonists. In his book "*Sic et non*" (Yes and No) the scholastic method was perfected. It was a product of Aristotelian logic and contributed much not only to the development of speculative theology but also to the progress of the deductive sciences and to the grammatical organization of the European languages.

Canute the Great: effective ruler who brought internal peace and prosperity to England. Strong supporter and generous donor to the church who brought Christian faith and culture to England and the Scandinavian countries.

1020s: as Danish king Canute was more and more involved in Danish affairs, long absence from England.
His deputies in England: Earl Thorkil of East Anglia, Godwin of Wessex.
Canute kept his own standing army of around 3,000 well-trained soldiers and levied an enormous amount of "Danegeld" (originally a contribution in order to finance the Anglo-Saxon army against the attacking Danes. Now became a permanent and general tax).

Saxon window

Easter 1027 pilgrimage to Rome, where he attended the coronation of Emperor Conrad II (religious and diplomatic motives). Canute secured reductions in toll for English pilgrims traders and from the Pope John XIX, Conrad II and other princes. English trade profited by Canute's control of the Baltic trade route and began to flourish (especially the cloth trade). A new class of English merchants emerged in the towns.

1027 Canute invaded Scotland and secured recognition from King Malcolm II.

1028 Canute became king of Norway, including Greenland, the Hebrides, Shetland and Orkney (until 1035).
Canute ✝ aged 40 **1035**
Buried in Winchester Cathedral. He wanted his legitimate son Hardecanute to succeed him on the English throne, but as H. was occupied with affairs as King of Denmark, the *Witan* (council of the Anglo-Saxons) appointed his eldest, but illegitimate son Harold Harefoot as new king.

Saxon doorway

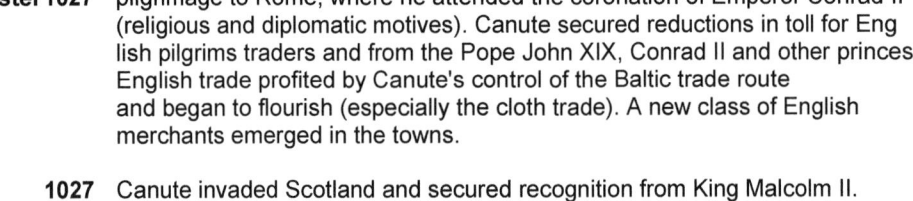

1036 Harold is responsible for the brutal murder of another royal claimant, Alfred the Aetheling, son of King Ethelred II the Unready (978-1016).
Harold banishes Hardecanute's

Mother and protects his realm from Welsh and Scottish invaders.

Saxon tower (Sompting church Sussex) with *German Helm* roof

Wulfstan 1002-23 Archbishop of York

1033 ✳ Anselm of Canterbury

Wulfstan ✝ 1023

Early Scholasticism:

1040 Harold Harefoot ✝ , successor: Hardecanute, son of Canute

    1042 ✝ Hardecanute (He died because he drank too much at a wedding!),
successor: Hardecanute's half brother Edward the Confessor,
son of Ethelred and Emma. Again an Anglo-Saxon becomes king.
Edward places friends from Normandy in high court and church positions. The
magnates are against this control. Therefore Godwin, Earl of Wessex, tries
to achieve a dominating position by the marriage of his daughter Edith to Edward.
Godwin succeeds; his sons Harold (Duke of Essex and East Anglia),
Tostig (Northumbria), and Sven (part of Mercia) soon have the power
in almost half of England.
Godwin becomes an outlaw later because of a refusal to obey a king's command
and is forced to leave the country with his family.

      1052 Godwin concentrates a fleet on the Flem-
ish coast. It unites with Harold's fleet and togeth
er they sail up the river Thames. When Kent joins
Godwin, Edward has to put him in his old position
as Earl of Wessex.

        1053 Godwin ✝
His son Harold Godwinson continues
Godwin's aims.

          Macbeth ✝ **1057**
The king of Scotland is killed in
the battle of Luphanan by
Malcolm III,. who later becomes
king

1050 Exeter Book is given to Exeter Cathedral by Bishop Leofric

1050 *Westminster Abbey*: Work starts to rebuilt the original
eighth century church (1050-1065) under Edward the
Confessor. This is the first example of the so-called Norman
Architecture in England.

        1058
Gloucester Cathedral: The benedectine
church is built.

Norman arcaded chapel, Tower of London

1040 ✳ **Reginald of Canterbury** *Vita St. Malachi*

1050 ✳ **Geoffrey of Winchester** *Epigrammata historica*
Norman builder

Norman Architecture:

Romanesque architecture developed in Normandy
and England between the 11th and the 12th centuries.
Characteristics of Norman architecture in England:
- massive constructions based on the rounded arch and
  on additive spatial compartmentalization
- longitudinal side-aisles and an apse or semi-circular
  projection of the eastern end of the centre aisle
- a raised nave with windows piercing the upper walls
- a triforium arcade, a western facade completed by two
  towers, and a central tower over the crossing with a
  square ground plan.

Early Scholasticism:

1060 Robert d'Oilly conquered Oxford
1065
Edward the Confessor ☦

1068 William quells revolts in north and west, lays the north waste
Westminster Abbey consecrated
1066
Witan offers throne to Harold II
1066 Appearance of Halley's Comet
1066 Tostig and Harold Haardraade of Norway invade northern England;
defeated at Stamford Bridge by Harold II.
William of Normandy (William the Conqueror) invades Sussex;
defeats and kills Harold II at Hastings and becomes king (until 1087)
14. Oct. Battle of Hastings
25. Dec. William of Normandy crowned as William I. of England in Westminster Abbey
Introduction of Feudalism after the Battle of Hastings
1066-87 *Windsor Castle*: Fortress built, founded by William I.
1066 *Tower of London*: White Tower built

1070 Bayeux tapestry, which tells the story of the Norman
invasion and conquest of England, is made.
1070 Malcolm III invades Northumbria
1070 Lanfranc becomes archbishop of Canterbury (to 1089)
1070 Hereward the Wake heads a rising in the fen country
1071 William subdues fen rebellion
1072 William raids Scotland
1073 Pope Gregory VII (to 1085)

First English Cluniac monastery is founded at Lewes, Sussex **1077**
Pope Gregory VII sends legates to reorganize church in England **1078**
1070 *Canterbury Cathedral*: Building of Norman church begun
after destruction of Saxon cathedral, architect: Archbishop
Lanfranc
1072 Building of *Lincoln Cathedral* begun
St. *Albans Cathedral* built of bricks from the ruins of Verulamium, (Romano-British town) in
1077

St. Albans Cathedral

The north transept (window designed and
erected by Lord Grimthorpe 19th cent.)
Arches and central tower by Paul of Caen
between 1077 and 1084
1065 ✳ **Eadmar of Canterbury** *Historia novorum in Anglia*

Building of *Rochester Cathedral* begun **1077**

Building of *Winchester Cathedral* begun **1079**
William's son Robert Curthose begins castle
which gives New-Castle-upon-Tyne its name
York Minster: Previous church burned and new
cathedral begun
1075 ✳ **Ordericus Vitalis**
Historia ecclesiastica

Feudalism:

A social system of rights and duties based on land tenure and personal relationships. According to feudalism, all the land of England belonged to the king, who - as the overlord - distributed parts of it as <u>fief</u> to loyal vassals called <u>barons</u>. In return, these vassals were bound to their overlord by their oath of allegiance. Furthermore, they had to perform military service for the king and owed him a certain number of fully armoured mounted soldiers. As this became increasingly expensive for the barons, they, too, decided to become feudal lords. Therefore they distributed parts of their land as fief to a lower group of vassals called <u>knights</u>. In return for their feudal tenure, the knights had to procure their horse and armour and fight for the king, alongside with the barons.

The Bayeux Tapestry
(medieval tapestry depicting the Norman conquest of England in more than 70 scenes, a band of linen 231ft long and 19.5 inches wide)

Early Scholasticism:

1082 William has his son Henry knighted
1086 William orders „Domesday Book".

Economic and tenurial record of England;

1087 ✝ William aged 60 on Sep. 9th
(killed by an arrow of a baron while hunting
- supposedly MURDER!!!)
succeeded by his son William II. (Rufus)
1089 William II waged war
on Normandy till 1096; subjugated it
1095
Call of Pope Urban II
for crusade **1099**
Capture of Jerusalem

1086 Domesday Book was made by order of William the Conqueror as a census record.
It surveyed ownership, area and values of lands and contains the numbers of tenants, live
stock and population.

1087 Building of *St. Paul's Cathedral* begun
1088 Building of *Tewkesbury Cathedral* begun
1089 *Gloucester Cathedral*: Early Norman rebuilding
1090 Building of *Ely Cathedral* begun
1092 *Lincoln Cathedral*: Norman church
consecrated
Building of *Durham Cathedral* **1093** begun
1096 Building of
Norwich Cathedral begun
1097-99
1080 ✳ **William of Malmesbury** *Historia novella*
Gesta pontificum Anglorum *Westminster Hall, Houses of Parliament*: lower part of the Hall built.
1084 ✳ **Henry of Huntingdon** *Historia Anglorum* **Durham Cathedral:** Choir and Crossing completed **1099**

English population in the 11th century:
Only five million acres of land were cultivated in the whole of England, the rest consisted mainly of woodland.
At that time England had only around 1.5 million inhabitants. They were living in scattered villages in the countryside or in small towns.
London at the end of the 11th century had c. 20,000 inhabitants, Lincoln, York, Norwich had over 5,000 inhabitants.
Most of the people living on the countryside were free peasants ("churls"), c. 9 % of the population were unfree villains.

Changes in English Literature after 1066

After the Norman conquest in 1066, the time of Old English Literature was near its end, the period of Middle English Literature had not yet started. In this time of change literature was not very important: "Literary Life" only began to develop again at the beginning of the 12th century. French was the language then spoken by the leading class, English was only spoken by the illiterate.
For this reason Old English Literature was no longer written down, but was only handed down by word of mouth. A consistency can be found through Chronicles which were continued until the mid-12th century (they show the language shift from Old English to Middle English clearly) and Homilies, which, in some regions, can also be found into the 12th century.

Bayeux Tapestry (1070)

Early Scholasticism:

1100 William II ✝ (was killed accidently or on purpose)
1100 Accession of Henry I (married Matilda, daughter of Malcolm III of Scotland)
youngest son of William I. Reconciles Anglo-Saxons and Normans by marriage
1100≈Foundation of the first guilds, merchants, goldsmiths, cloth merchants)
1100 Charta Liberatum was drafted (predecessor of Magna Charta Liberatum)
    1103 Anselm of Canterbury went into exile again (archbishop of Canterbury, first scholastic theologian)
        1107 Agreement between Henry I and Church in investiture matters
(Canterbury Concordat)
        1107 Investiture contest was ended
Anselm of Canterbury ✝   **1109** (Father of Scholasticism)
        1109 Henry I at war with Louis IV of France
                1114 Matilda, daughter of Henry I mar
                -ried Henry V, the Holy Roman Emperor
                Leges Henrici, a collection of
                laws, were made   **1118**
                Matilda, wife of Henry I ✝   **1118**

1100 - 1490 *Chester Cathedral*

                1116 *Peterborough Cathedral* was burned
                1117 reconstruction begun

Anselm of Canterbury ✝ 1109
Reginald of Canterbury ✝ 1109
Geoffrey ofWinchester ✝ 1107

1100 ✳ Geoffrey of Monmouth,

Henry VIII gave Peterborough cathedral status in 1541; it had been one of the great Benedictine abbey churches, but the abbey was dissolved in 1539. The site was first consecrated in 655, when the King of Mercia founded a Benedictine monastery there. This was sacked by the Danes in 870, and a second monastery was destroyed by fire in 116. The present building was started by the Abbot Jean de Seez. Apart from its west front, Peterborough is an outstanding example of the Norman-Romanesque style. The Benedictines, conservative in their architecture, carried on building in this style up to the last decade of the 12th century - more than 20 years after England's first truly Gothic buildings had made their appearance.

Peterborough Cathedral WEST FRONT

Thomas Becket ✳**1118**

Literature:	Anselm of Canterbury 1033-1109:	*Cur deus homo*?
	Reginald of Canterbury1040-1109:	*Vita St. Malchi*
	Geoffrey of Winchester 1050-1107:	*Epigrammata historica*
	Eadmar of Canterbury 1065-1124?:	*Historica novorum in Anglia*
	Geoffrey of Monmouth 1100?-1154:	*Historica regum Britanniae* (deals with the legend of King Arthur)
		Vita Merlini(1148)
	Ordericus Vitalis 1075-.1142:	*Historia ecclesiastica* (deals with the history of the Normans)
	William Malm(e)sbury 1080-1142?:	*Historia* (or *Gesta*) *regum Anglorum* (English history of kings 449-1127)
		Historia novella (English history 1125-1142)
		Gesta pontificum Anglorum
	Henry of Huntingdon 1084-1155:	*Historia Anglorum* (British history 55 B.C.- 1155)

| 1120 | Henry I | 1135 Stephen of Blois | 1140 |

| 1120 | 1121 | 1122 | 1123 | 1124 | 1125 | 1126 | 1127 | 1128 | 1129 | 1130 | 1131 | 1132 | 1133 | 1134 | 1135 | 1136 | 1137 | 1138 | 1139 | 1140 |

| 1120 | 1124 | David I | 1140 |

Early Scholasticism:

1120 ✝ Prince William, heir to the throne, drowned
1120 Peace between Henry I and Louis VI of France
1120 ✳ John of Salisbury, Historian and Philosopher
 1122 Henry makes his illegitimate son Robert de Caen Earl of Gloucester
 1122 ✳ Eleonor of Aquitaine, future wife of Henry II, married to the French king Louis VII in **1137**
Alexander I of Scotland ✝ **1124** **1227** Henry I persuades his barons to accept his
 daughter Matilda as heir to the English throne
 1128 widowed Matilda marries Geoffrey Plantagenet,
 son of the Count of Anjou
 1130 Innocent II becomes Pope

 1135 Stephen de Blois,
 grandson of William I,
 becomes King of
 England against the
 claims of Matilda,
 daughter of Henry I.
 Stephen victorious in battles against the Scots **1138**
 Quarrels between the magnates **1138**
 CIVIL WAR

Architecture
Early English (also: Lancet Style) up to 1270, parallel:Gothic architecture influenced by France.
 1128 England's first Cistercian monastery founded at Waverly, Surrey
 1123 *St. Bartholomew Church* in London built **1131** Tintern Abbey (Wales) founded
 1123 - (1419) *Carlisle Cathedral* (decorated choir 1292-1362)
 1123 *Tewkesbury Cathedral* built in Norman style
 1130 *Church of the Holy Sepulchre*
 1132 (-1500) *Fountain Abbey*
 (Cistercian Monastery)
 1133 *Durham Cathedral* (important parts
 of the finest Norman building were
 finished)
 1136 *Glasgow Cathedral*
 begun

Melrose Abbey was founded by David I in 1136 for monks brought from Rievaulx in Yorkshire. The location on a site in the valley of the Tweed was ideal for sheep farming, which produced a large part of the abbey's income, and nearby Berwick provided a convenient market for the monks to sell their wool. The house was close to the main road from England to Edinburgh, and so received visits from many eminent people whose donations made it one of the wealthiest abbeys in Scotland.
But it was near the border where constant warring between England and Scotland occurred. In 1385 the troops of Richard II sacked the abbey seriously enough to warrant rebuilding of the church. This is now the main survival, largely because it was used as a parish church until 1810.
It has many features or northern English architecture. For instance, the facades of the south and east arms compare with the west and east facades of York Minster (14th cent.)
It was a splendid church, and its reconstruction lasted into the 16th century. But in 1547 Melrose was again sacked by the English under the Duke of Somerset, and never recovered.

Melrose Abbey (Cistercian) 1136
sacked by Edward II in 1322 and Richard II in 1385

1120 ✳ **John of Salisbury**, Historian and Philosopher

 1130 ? ✳ **Nigel Wireker**, *Brunellus sive speculum stultorum*
 1126 Adelard of Bath translated astronomical tables of al-Khwarizmi from Arabic into Latin

1140	Stephen of Blois	1154 Henry II	1160

1140 1141 1142 1143 1144 1145 1146 1147 1148 1149 1150 1151 1152 1153 1154 1155 1156 1157 1158 1159 1160

1140	David I	1153	1160

Early Scholasticism:

1141 Battle of Lincoln, Matilda forces Stephen's capture (Stephen and Robert, Earl of Gloucester, exchanged)

1147-1149 Second Crusade, ended in military disaster

1147 ●Faversham Abbey, Kent, founded by Henry, son of Matilda

●Henry invaded England unsuccessfully

1148 Matilda left England

1149 Henry returned to England; knighted by David I of Scotland

1152 Henry of Anjou (later Henry II) ∞ Eleanor of Aquitaine

1153 Civil war ended

1154 ●Nicholas Breakspear elected as Pope Adrian IV

1140 1141 1142 1143 1144 1145 1146 1147 1148 1149 1150 1151 1152 1153 1154 1155 1156 1157 1158 1159 1160

Stephen of Blois ✝ **1154**

1154 ●Henry II becomes King of England

●Henry appointed Thomas Becket Lord Chancellor

1140 *St Patrick's Purgatory*

1143 first translation of the Koran into Latin by Robert of Chester

1157 Henry forced Malcolm IV of Scotland to give up Nortumberland, Cumberland and Westmorland

1143 *Durham Cathedral* completed, 1093 ⇐

Bernard of Clairvaux ✝ **1153**

1157 ✳ Richard I (1091 ✳), founded Cistercian monasteries

Norman and Romanesque Architecture

Church of SS Mary and David, Kilpeck (Herefs.) 1145 (Norman) **1151** The game of chess came to England

English territories in France in the 12th century

Early Scholasticism:

1162 Becket was consecrated bishop
and enthroned as Archbischop of Canterbury
Disputes about appointments to bishoprics, and on the subject of separate church courts
Opposition to taxes imposed by Henry.

1164 Council and Constitutions (16) of Clarendon, regarded as direct attack
on the rights of the Church by Becket
Council at Nottingham: Becket repudiated his original agreement
1164, 2nd November, Becket goes into exile
1166 Becket finds hospitality in the monastery of St. Colombe, Sens
1166 Assize of Clarendon
1167✳ John I, brother of Richard I.
1169(-1172) English Conquest of Ireland begins
1170, June 14 coronation of Prince Henry by the Archbishop of
York, thus defying the orders and rights of Thomas Becket
1170, July   Short lived reconciliation with King Henry

Thomas Becket   ✝ **1170**, December 29th, murdered in Canterbury Cathedral
probably caused by Henry II
1173, February 21st, official canonization of
Becket by Pope Alexander III

1171   ●Henry II claims dominion over Ireland
●papal consent achieved
1173-74   ●Rebellion against Henry II
●William the Lion, king of

Orford Castle   Scotland invades the north

Architecture Norman Style

1174   Quire of Canterbury Cathedral
burnt out

Oxford Cathedral built in perpendicular style **1175**
Rebuilding of *Canterbury Cathedral* in perpendicular style   **1178**
1166 Mysteries and Miracle Plays performed in London churches
1170 John of Tilbury, *Nova Ars Notaria*, short-hand system

Built in the 12th century for Henry II, Orford Casle was intended to curtail the power of turbulent
East Anglian barons, such as Hugh Bigod of nearby Framlingham Castle. Its polygonal keep was built
to a revolutionary design, which is today a landmark in the Suffolk landscape. This unconventional
design is matched by an unusual history, marked by drama of all kinds.

1175 ✳ **Alexander of Hales**,
Aristotelian philosopher

below: Becket embarking for England (1st December, 1170)
underneath: messengers tell him of the arrival of the four knights   below: The martyrdom in a painting 20 or 30 years later

Early Scholasticism:

1181 First Carthusian monastery in England founded at Witham, Somerset

1186 Henry II makes peace with Phillip II of France
1186 3rd Crusade began

Henry II ✝ **1189**
1189 ●Richard I the Lionheart succeeds him
●Massacre of Jews at Richard´s coronation
●Richard, third son of Henry II, forces his father
to make him heir to the throne (together with
Phillip II of France)

1190 Richard I on Crusade
1191 English crusaders reach Palestine

1192 ●**Treaty between Richard and Saladin**
●End of the 3rd Crusade but:
Leopold of Austria captures Richard
While he was imprisoned his brother
John claimed the throne.
1193 94 Richard in prison in Germany

1194 Richard I pays ransom to
Heinrich VI and is released
from being held hostage.
Plymouth navy base **1199**

1180 1181 1182 1183 1184 1185 1186 1187 1188 1189 1190 1191 1192 1193 1194 1195 1196 1197 1198 1199 1200

Richard I ✝1199

Architecture: Norman Style turning into Early English

Dover Castle

Lincoln Cathedral

1180 Glass windows introduced in England
1180-86 *Dover Castle*, Keep by Henry II, inside are the Pharos and St. Mary, a Saxon church.

1192 **Lincoln Cathedral**, English Gothic, partially
destroyed by earthquake in 1185

Lincoln became the centre of a bishopric in 1072, when the See was transferred from Dorchester (Oxfordshire). A cathedral was begun at once, but much of the present church dates from after an earthquake in 1185. It has been little altered since its completion about 1280. Lincoln has had one of the most varied successions of bishops of any English See. Among them were Alexander the Magnificent (1123-48), the illegitimate son of the influential royal servant, Bishop Roger of Salisbury, who was probably responsible for the Romanesque parts of the west front; St Hugh of Avalon (1186 - 1200), an ascetic Carthusian, brought unwillingly from his monastery, and Robert Grosseteste (1235-53), a strong supporter of Oxford University in its early years, when it fell within the Diocese of Lincoln. Inside the cathedral, St Hugh's choir and nave are impressive examples of early Gothic architecture, with fine columns of Purbeck stone. To the east, the Angel Choir is one of the most heavily decorated of its period. The whole interior is dominated by the immense traceried window in the east end.

1180 John of Salisbury ✝ , Historian and philosopher wrote
Thomas Becket´s biography
Metalogicus and *Polycraticus*

1180 1181 1182 1183 1184 1185 1186 1187 1188 1189 1190 1191 1192 1193 1194 1195 1196 1197 1198 1199 1200

High Scholasticism:

1203 Philip Augustus conquers Anjou and Normandy

Prince Arthur ✝ **1203** Prince Arthur, the rightful heir to the English throne, is murdered.
The Pope demands King Philip of France to the throne.

1204
● Normandy becomes French.
● Philip II. snatches away the duchy from England.

1208 - 1214 **Interdict:** Churches are closed, no masses.
King John is excommunicated.

1213 King John I. submits to the Pope.

Battle of Bouvines. King Philipp II. defeats King John I **1214**.

The Barons in arms force King John to sign the **Magna Charta**. **1215**

King John I ✝ **1216** in a war against the Barons.
1216 Henry III. is pro claimed King of England at the age of nine. He marries Eleanor of Provence.

1200 The *University of Cambridge* is built.

1204 The *Cathedral of Lincoln* is renovated in gothic style.

1209 *First stone bridge crossing the Thames in London*

On a splendid natural site, almost surrounded by the Pembroke River, this castle became a fortress in the settlement of Wales in the late 11th century. The magnificent round keep and inner bailey date from about 1200.

The 13th-century curtain walls are light, the steep banks to the river themselves forming a defence. The castle's dilapidated condition was largely the result of an epic siege by Cromwell's troops in 1648.

Pembroke Castle

Magna Carta Libertatum (Medieval Latin for "Great Charter of Freedoms"), commonly called Magna Carta (also Magna Charta; "Great Charter"),[a] is a royal charter[4][5] of rights agreed to by King John of England at Runnymede, near Windsor, on 15 June 1215.[b] First drafted by Archbishop of Canterbury Stephen Langton to make peace between the unpopular king and a group of rebel barons, it promised the protection of church rights, protection for the barons from illegal imprisonment, access to swift justice, and limitations on feudal payments to the Crown, to be implemented through a council of 25 barons. Neither side stood behind their commitments, and the charter was annulled by Pope Innocent III, leading to the First Barons' War.

After John's death, the regency government of his young son, Henry III, reissued the document in 1216, stripped of some of its more radical content, in an unsuccessful bid to build political support for their cause. At the end of the war in 1217, it formed part of the peace treaty agreed at Lambeth, where the document acquired the name Magna Carta, to distinguish it from the smaller Charter of the Forest which was issued at the same time. Short of funds, Henry reissued the charter again in 1225 in exchange for a grant of new taxes. His son, Edward I, repeated the exercise in 1297, this time confirming it as part of England's statute law. The charter became part of English political life and was typically renewed by each monarch in turn, although as time went by and the fledgling Parliament of England passed new laws, it lost some of its practical significance.

Architecture: Early English Style

Roger Bacon, English philosopher ✴ **1215**

~ **1200** **an.**, *The Vices and Virtues*: (First middle English poetic dialogue between "Good sense and soul")

1206 Layamon translates Wace's verse chronicle *Roman de Brut* into English and enlarges it by 20.000 lines

1212 Gervasius of Tilbury, *Otia imperialia*, geography and history of England

High Scholasticism:

1221-1224 Arrival of Dominican and Franciscan Friars in England
1224 Louis VIII completes conquest of Poitou

✳ Edward I. **1239**
(King of England from 1272 - 1307)

1215 **Passages from the Magna Carta:**
 17. Ordinary lawsuits shall not follow the royal court around, but shall be held in a fixed place.
 20. For a trivial offence, a free man shall be fined only in proportion to the degree of his offence, and for a serious offence correspondingly, but not so heavily as to deprive him of his livelihood. In the same way, a merchant shall be spared his merchandise, and a husband implements of his husbandry, if they fall upon the mercy of a royal court.
 None of these shall be imposed except by the assessment of the reputable men of the neighbourhood.

1220 *Saint Edmund Hall College* founded in Oxford
1220 Oxford opens first University Building: *St. Edmund Hall*
1220 Beginning of the construction of *Salisbury Cathedral*
 1221 Westside of the *Cathedral of Peterborough* (Anglo-Norman Style)

Architecture: Early English Style

Salisbury Cathedral (1220 - 1258)

The Norman cathedral was at what is now Old Sarum, where its plan can still be seen in the grass, but at the start of the 13th century the See was moved to New Sarum, or Salisbury. The present cathedral is the only English one built in the Middle Ages as a single conception, and not piecemeal as were all the others. The foundations were laid in 1220, and about 60 years later this magnificent Early English cathedral was finished. Its spire was added in 1334. There are many interesting monuments, including the spectacular brass to Bishop Wyville, c. 1375, who is shown standing in a castle. The main decorative elements inside the cathedral are the dark columns of Purbeck stone which appear throughout the building. In the 14th century Edward III granted a licence to build a wall round the cathedral and the houses of those who served it, and much of this wall surrounding the close survives.

The story of how the cathedral spire was built was fictionalised by William Golding. His novel *The Spire* was published in 1964

Thomas De Hales, *Luve Ron.*(Religious poems) **~1240**
Hali Meidenhead, *Holy Virgin* (Glorification of Chastity) **1st** half of **13th** cen.

High Scholasticism:

1240 Llywelyn the Great ✝

1254 Henry III accepts papal offer of throne of Sicily

Misgovernment. The Baron's war 1258 - 1260

Treaty of Paris between England and France 1259

Parliament is a feudal court
Writs to sheriffs summoned:

bishops ⎫
abbots ⎪
7 earls ⎬ Parliament met at unregular times
2 burgesses ⎪ as an occasion for transacting
41 barons ⎪ important and public business
2 citizens ⎭ in consultation with his great men.

Provisions of Oxford 1258

Barons take over royal government
- 12 men, elected by the communitas, have to attend Parl.
- Communitas will ratify everything that is done by the twelve in advance.

The term *Parliament* becomes firmly established in the Chancery rolls.

Introduction of general and uniform taxes,
including tree tenants as well as systematic taxation of movables.

Terms and Definitions: (German translations in italics)

King's bench	one of three High Courts	knightly association	*Ritterbund*
estate	*Stand*	convocation	*Provinzialsynode*
realm of estates	*Ständestaat*	Canon Law	*Kirchenrecht*
vill	*Ortseinheit* ⇒ villains	borough	*Ortschaft m. Parl.vertretung*
shire	*Grafschaft*	burgess	representative of borough in P.
hundred	*Verwaltungseinheit (Heer)*	guild	*Handwerkerinnung*
folkmoot	*Volksversammlung*	forfeiture	loss of property as punishment
attainder	legal forfeiture of property + civil rights		

Growth of Representation:
1110 the vill
1166 the shire
1166 the hundred
1226 the cathedral chapter
1254 the diocesan clergy
1258 the barons
1258 community of the land
1265 the borough   **York Minster**

Architecture: Early English Style

1215-1260 South and north transepts of York Cathedral are built in Early English Style, finished 1472
1240 Construction of the *Temple Church in London* finished.
1240 *Temple Church* in London completed
1245 *Westminster Abbey* in London

Cathedral of Salisbury consecrated in **1258**
(Early English Style)

1240 1241 1242 1243 1244 1245 1246 1247 1248 1249 1250 1251 1252 1253 1254 1255 1256 1257 1258 1259 1260

1242 **Roger Bacon** reports about gunpowder, which had been invented in China in the 12th century.
Alexander of Hales ✝ **1245**, Summa universae theologiae

1250 The **English** language has reached the **same cultural level as French or Latin**.
1250-1300 In the Irish Abbey Kildare *The Land of Cockaygne* is **written by a travelling cleric**. It is a revision of a French model.
1250 *The Fox and the Wolf*, satirical verse poetry
1250 *The Land of Cokaygne*, from Kildare Abbey

High Scholasticism:

Edward I, eldest son of Henry III, born at Westminster in 1239, married (1) Eleanor, daughter of Ferdinand III of Castile; (2) Margaret, daughter of Philip III of France, died at Burgh near Carlisle 7 July 1307

1262 Llywelyn of Wales **invades England**.
1263 ●King Henry III. is released from his oath in Rome.
●**Town-and-Gown riot** in Oxford.

1264 ●May, Henry III defeated by **Simon de Montfort**
Henry III and Prince Edward are captured
●June, Parliament (Forma Pacis - Forma Regiminis)
1265 Simon de Montfort's Reform of Parliament
Two knights from every county, two citizens or burgesses from every city and
borough summoned: Forerunner of representative parliament.
1265 August, Battle of Evesham: Prince Edward escapes from Welsh captivity and defeats Simon de Montfort with reactivated troops. Simon is killed in action.

1268 ●Prince Edward convenes a parliament following the model
parliament of S. de Montfort.   Church ⅂
●**Edward confirms the Magna Charta** and the liberty of the

1270-1274 Prince **Edward leads a crusade** which is less
successful. Edward survives only by chance.
Henry III ✞ **November** **1272**.
1272 Edward is proclaimed as King in absence. He does not return until 1274.

1274 King Edward I. reduces the
power of the Barons and
increases the parliament. He
organizes the taxes and the
military.

King Edward I invades Wales and drives Llywelyn back to the Snowdon **1277**

Justice: „Four knights" system of gaol delivery abandoned

1260-1285 Octagonal *Chapter House of the York Cathedral* is built in Decorated Style.

Roger Bacon (1214 - 1294), Franciscan Friar, scientist and natural philosopher advocates the experimental method.

Architecture: Decorated Style

climax of High Scholasticism due to:
●new ideas from Aristoteles and Arabic philosophers
●union of the schools to form universities
●step forward in scientific life of the Dominicans and Franciscans

Three directions:
1. *conservative Augustinism* **vs.**
2. *Latin Averroism*
3. *Aristotelism of Albertus Magnus* and *Thomas von Aquino* (finally dominated)
then:
Thomism **vs**. the *young Franciscan school of Duns Scotus*
People like **Roger Bacon** (scientifically orientated) and the close **connection between scholastic and mystic** were important for this development.

1260-1300 In the Gloucester Abbey, **Robert of Gloucester** writes an epic poem in 12,000 verses about British history

1280 Alexander III 1286 Margaret 1290 / 1292 John de Balliol 1296 /1300

High Scholasticism:

1282 ●**David,** brother of Llywelyn of Wales, **leads a rebellion against England.**
●**Edward I defeats the Welsh**, Llywelyn is killed in action; David is hanged.
1283 **Wales conquered by Edward I**
1283 **King Edward I rules over Wales.**
1284 ✸ **Edward II** (King of England 1307 - 1327)
1285 Statute of Winchester regulates the organization
of police and defence. Communities and districts now
have to care for inner safety, road construction and local police.
Everyone holding land worth £ 15 a year has to maintain a knight and horse.
1286 **King Alexander III. of Scotland dies** after having united the country.

Princess Margaret of Scotland ✞ 1290 The heir to the Scottish throne, **Princess Margaret dies on the journey to Scotland**. The Scottish Barons demand King Edward I to proclaim a new Scottish King.

Eleonor of Castile ✞ 1290 ●**King Edward I stops the realisation of a new crusade** because of the death of his wife Eleonor.
● **Expulsion of the Jews** after 100 years of persecution.
1292 **King Edward I proclaims John Balliol as the Scottish King.** Scotland becomes dependent on England until 1328.

King Edward I conquers Wales after a rebellion.**1294**

1295 **Model Parliament**
Commons + Barons in
●**A rebellion** by the Scots **against John Balliol is ended by King Edward I 1298**
●He defeats the Scots in Falkirk and burns down Perth and St. Andrews.

Royal Assizes: 2 justices of assize to hold sessions in the counties at least three times a year
Civil + criminal trials = system of dual-purpose circuit justice.

| **Common Law Courts** | | |
| Court of King's Bench | Court of Common Pleas | Court of Exchequer |

Lord Chief Justice highest permanent judge of the Crown
1289 Judicial commissions appointed
Edward to try corrupt justices,
exchequer officials and sheriffs.
1283 *Caernarvon Castle* built
1285 *Conway Castle* built
1291 Building of *York Cathedral* begins

Architecture: Early English turning into Decorated Style

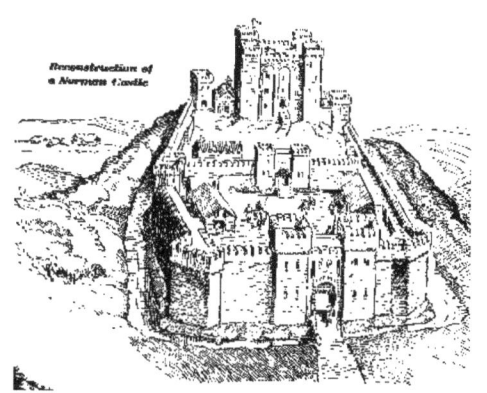

1290 ✸ **William of Ockham**, philosopher, nominalist
Roger Bacon ✞ **1294**

| 1300 | Edward I | 1307 | Edward II | 1320 |

| 1300 | 1301 | 1302 | 1303 | 1304 | 1305 | 1306 | 1307 | 1308 | 1309 | 1310 | 1311 | 1312 | 1313 | 1314 | 1315 | 1316 | 1317 | 1318 | 1319 | 1320 |

| 1300 John de Balliol 1306 | Robert (I) Bruce | 1320 |

Late Scholasticism:

Edward II, *son of Edward I, born at Carnarvon 1284, married Isabella, daughter of Philip IV of France, deposed Jan. 20, 1327, murdered in Berkeley Castle, Sept. 21, 1327.*

1306   **Rebellion of Robert Bruce**

1306   Robert I Bruce King of Scotland

Edward I ✝ 1307

1307 **Accession of Edward II**

1305   **Lent Parliament**
95 prelates
145 representatives of the inferior clergy
9 earls
94 barons
74 knights of the shires
200 citizens and burgesses
Total = 600
1307 **Statute of Carlisle**
Petition of the magnates and community relief of taxation

1313 **England exports 30.000 sacks of wool, 5000 pieces of cloth**
   1314 **Scottish victory at Bannockburn**
   1314 **Scotland gains independence from England**
   Great famine   **1315-1316**

The business of Parliament:

Maitland: „ ... that a session of the king's council is the core and essence of every parliamentum. ... Primarily a parliament is a high court of justice."
No financial supply was asked for, none was granted. The summoning of parliament was a measure required not by the crown so much as by its subjects.

1. the discussion of affairs of state, more especially

2. legislation

3. taxation or supply

4. the audience of peti-

5. judicial business, the determination of causes

Lower Exchequer: Accounting department, government office, permanent treasury
Upper Exchequer: Court to sit twice a year to regulate accounts, made up by barons, officials and accountants

Architecture: Decorated Style

Chancery - Exchequer: Petitions consisted of five bundles:
- one for the chancery
- another one for the exchequer
- a third one for the justices
- a fourth one for the king and his council
- the fifth containing those which had already been answered

1300 ✸William of Ockham

Duns Scotus ✝ **1308**, Scholastic philosopher

Middle English Literature

North East (Lincolnshire)
Mysticism of Richard Rolle

**West (Worcestershire) and
North-West (Lancashire)**
Langland and alleg. dream visions
social and religious tensions

Middle England (Oxford)
Wyclif's bible translations
reform movements

South-East (London)

1320	EDWARD II	1327		EDWARD III	1340

1320 1321 1322 1323 1324 1325 1326 1327 1328 1329 1330 1331 1332 1333 1334 1335 1336 1337 1338 1339 1340

1320	Robert (I)Bruce	1329	David II	1340

Late Scholasticism:

1324 **William of Ockham** invited to Avignon because he favoured the separation of state and church. To evade inquisition he fled to Munich

1326 Scottish Parliament founded, Robert I called estates together to finance war

1327 ●Regime of favourites under Edward I

●Summonses (three per year) by individual writs through bishops and sheriffs

●Deposition of Edward II (successful revolt in1327)

●Election of Edward III by magnates and acclamation by populos, not by Parliament.

1328 England acknowledges Scottish independence

1328 ●Treaty of Northampton (England accepts Scotland`s inde pendence)

●End of Capetidynasty in France followed by fight about succession to the throne of France prelude to the Hundred Years´ War (1339- 1454)

●Statute of 1328: Charters of pardon only in cases of self-defence and homicide by misadventure

●Legislation: heavy taxation, purveyance misused, lords and commons reluctant to finance the French War

Orientation in Society

The change of economic conditions in the early Middle Ages produces a sense of common interest amongst equals and leads to the formation of associations and the organization of society by estates.

1330 Edward III introduces Judges of the Peace.

1330 ●Statute of 1330: change of liability after a debtor`s death - successor becomes responsible.
clergy an order apart; spiritual property not subject to taxation unless they gave their consent

●Statute prescribing annual parliaments (514 members; "Common People of an Earldom" were not yet a separate part of parliament - they organ-ised petitions or bills)

52 Spiritual lords (21 bishops, 31 abbots)

77 Temporal lords (11 earls, 66 barons)

10 Councillors (centre of government; judges, advisors of the king.)

74 knights of the shires (elected in county courts by stewards and bailiffs)

1333 Barons of the exchequer on the bor der between law and finance

1335 Economic situation: increasing economic depres-sion, heavy taxation, scarcity of money, low food prizes – de-cline in the purchasing power, deflationary situation

1320 1321 1322 1323 1324 1325 1326 1327 1328 1329 1330 1331 1332 1333 1334 1335 1336 1337 1338 1339 1340

Architecture: Decorated Style turning into Perpendicular Style

Six assize circuits: Home, Midland, Norfolk, Oxford, Northern, Western **1337**

1324 **Nave and aisle of York Cathedral built in Decorated Style.**

Edward III claims French throne **1339**
⇓ **Anglo- French War until 1453**
Edward III is also king of France **1339**
1336 Chichester Cath. finished

1321 Queen Mary Psalter (Engl. book painting) **1328** ✹ **John Wycliffe,** Reformer and Bible translator

William v. Occam (1300 -1350) Franciscan; prepared the separation between faith and science, the basis of Re-naissance philosophy **1330** ✹ **John Gower**

In the 14 th century:
Heyday of medieval English poetry
●**North East - Lincolnshire: mystics around Richard Rolle (?1290-1349)**
●**William Langley (1332-1400):** *Piers Plowman* **(allegorical dream poetry; expresses the social and religious ten-sion of the time**
(also: Langland)

Robert Mannyng, *The History of England* **1337**
Richard Rolle, *Incendium amoris*, **mysticist** **1339**

Late Scholasticism:

Hundred Years War
1340 The **English beat the French** at the battle of Sluys
1340 Merchant navy victorious over French fleet
1340/1341 Armistices between Edward III and Philip VI
1341 The **English are driven out of Scotland**
1345 ●Bohun, **Earl of Northampton conquers Brittany**
1345 ●Philipps break of the armistice leads **Edward** to **sending troops to the Gascoigne and Brittany**.
●**In Crecy-en-Ponthieu Edward wins** a great battle
1346 **The English beat the French at Abbeville (Crecy)**
1346 David of Scotland captured by the English
1347-1350 **One fifth of the English population dies of the plague**
1348 **Plague in London and Europe**
1348 Order of the Garter created
Edward moves into Aquitaine and loots the area along the Loire **1356**

1350 Division of Parliament into
House of Lords and *House of Commons*
1351 Tennis becomes open air lawn game
1355 In a battle between citizens, students and lecturers of Oxford **100 students are** As a punishment the town has to pay money to the university until 1825

Treaty of Berwick: **1357** David II of Scotland is released for a ransom of 100.000 Marks, payable over 10 years; a cause of high taxation to impoverished Scotland in years to come.

Architecture: Decorated Style(until ~1350) / Perpendicular Style (1350-~1500)
1350 *Windsor Castle* rebuilt by Edward III
St.-Nicholas-Cathedral in Newcastle built in Perpendicular style **1359**
1349 English language gains predominance over Norman French in schools

William of Occam, nominalist ✝ **1349**
1340 ✳**Geoffrey Chaucer** (✝1400)
Richard Rolle of Hampole ✝ **1349** (✳1290)

Four cycles
1340-1350 *The York Plays, The Townely Plays (Wakefield);* **1350** *The Chester Plays; Ludus Coventriae = Hegge Plays*

The Pilgrim's Way

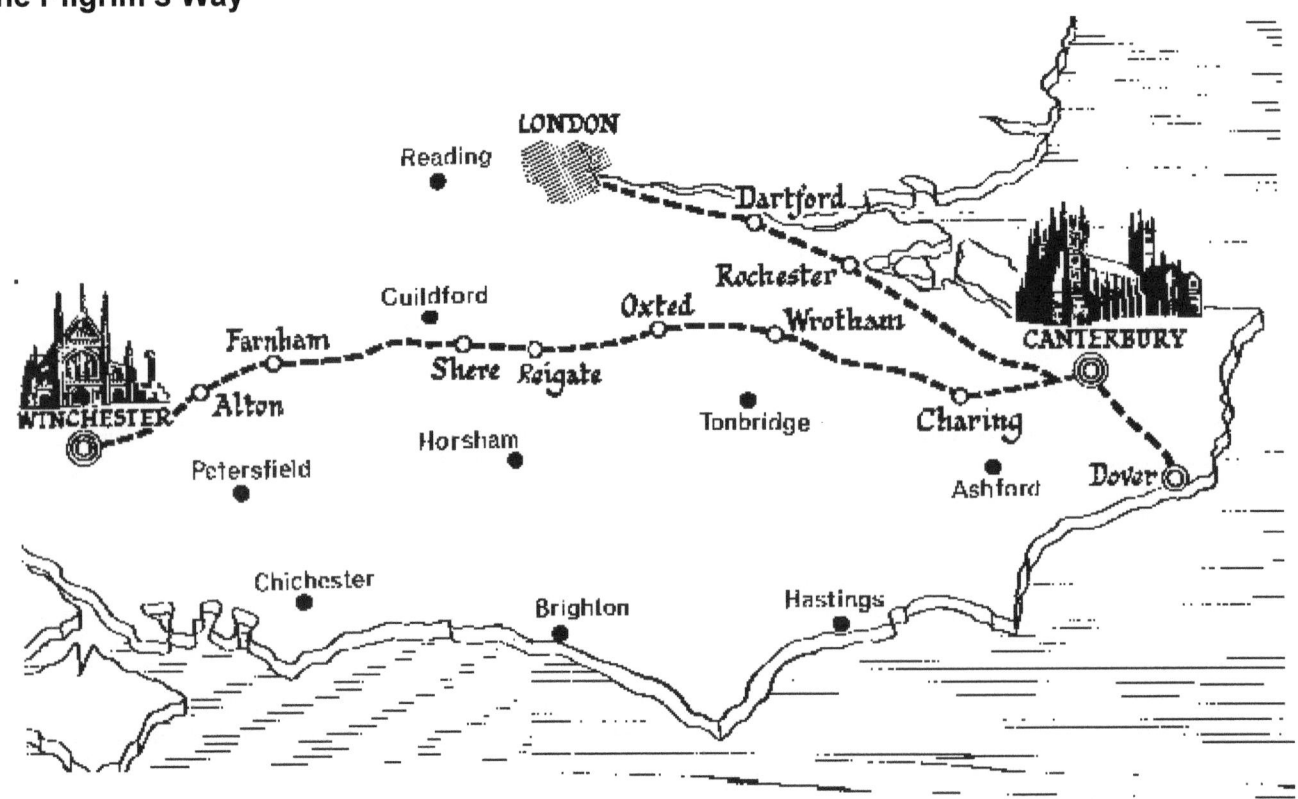

1360	Edward III	1377 Richard II 1380

1360 1361 1362 1363 1364 1365 1366 1367 1368 1369 1370 1371 1372 1373 1374 1375 1376 1377 1378 1379 1380

1360	David II	1371	Robert II	1380

Late Scholasticism:

Richard II, son of Edward the Black Prince, born at Bordeaux, 1367, married (1) Anne, daughter of Charles IV of Bohemia; (2) Isabella, daughter of Charles VI of France, deposed Sept. 29, 1399, said to have been murdered in Pontefract Castle,Feb.1400.

1360 Contract of Brétigny: Edward III renounces his claims to the French throne   Edward ☦ **1377**

1362 "Statute of Pleaders" English becomes official language of law-courts

1364 Battle of Auray   1369 Edward III resumes the title King of France

1367-69 The Black Prince **(Edward) fights battles**
                        involving heavy losses **against Castile**

1348 - 1369   **"Black Death"** reduces population by a quarter;
                        one fifth of the villages disappears

1370 Wycliffe in Oxford, opposes celibacy, papal supremacy
1371 Stuarts hold the Scottish throne

**1374/5   No Parliaments were
                        held**

Great Schism 1378-1417

Architecture: Perpendicular Style

England suffers a defeat with high losses **against** the fleet of **Castile and France 1379**

1376 Good Parliament

Architecture:
  Picture: *Hardwick Hall*, Derbyshire, England
  (1360-1550) Perpendicular style

„every great change made in parliament was due to the initiative of the commons expressed through their chosen speaker." unanimity of orders

1369   *Exeter Cathedral* finished in High Perpendicular style

1369 ✳ **John Dunstable**, Engl. Composer

Apsis and choir of *Gloucester Cathedral* finished **1377**

1340?-1400 Geoffrey Chaucer actual founder of English poetry
1340- 1399 John of Gaunt, 4th son of Edward; dominant figure of the royal family
1330?-1408 John Gower, poet and respected scholar at the British court,(*Confessio amantis* 1390)

1372 Oxford becomes intellectual centre of England

William Langley (1332-1400) greatest poet after Chaucer in the Middle Ages, „*Piers Plowman*"**1378/79**
                        (allegorical dream poetry; expresses the social and religious tension of that time)

1370?   **„Gawain"-poet** (unknown):*Pearl; Cleanness; Pacience; Sir Gawayne and the Green Knight*

Robin Hood mentioned in ballad   **1377**
John Wycliffe(1320-1384) got into conflict with the church hierarchy ●*De civili dominio*   **1377/78** "
                                                                    ●*De ecclesia*
                                                                    ●*De officio regis*

| 1380 | Richard II | 1399 Henry IV | 1400 |

| 1380 | 1381 | 1382 | 1383 | 1384 | 1385 | 1386 | 1387 | 1388 | 1389 | 1390 | 1391 | 1392 | 1393 | 1394 | 1395 | 1396 | 1397 | 1398 | 1399 | 1400 |

| 1380 | Robert II | 1390 | Robert III | 1400 |

Humanism

1381 **Peasants´ revolt** (due to increase in poll tax) **led by Wat Tyler and John Ball** "When Adam delved and Eve span, who was then the gentleman?"

1382 Foundation of the "Public School"

Richard II

1388 **"Merciless Parliament"**; the "Lords Appellant", summoned by rebels. accuse the King´s friends of treason , The king's supporters executed, exiled or imprisoned.
A 25-year peace treaty with France **1396**; secured by the **marriage of Richard and the French King´s daughter Isabella of Valois.**

The lords of the "Merciless Parliament" are accused, **the acts of 1388 are annulled in 1397**

Banishment of Henry Bolingbroke **1398**

Parliament confirms Richard`s forced resignation **30. September** **1399**

The first Lancastrian, **Henry Bolingbroke, becomes King of Britain** **1399**

At the end of the 14th century the sheriffs lost a lot of their power; their office was taken over by *justices of the peace*; they became the judicial authority on the local level. Parliament was the highest judicial institute, important for financial matters. The king could no more rule without parliament.

Architecture: High Perpendicular

Travellers of medieval roads

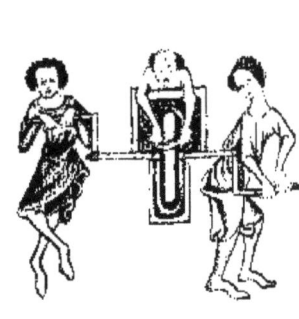

The showman and his bear   **Minstrels, jugglers, charlatans**   **A pilgrim**   **grinders**
from: Trevelyan. *Illustrated English Social History*: vol.1, p.98 f.

1381 Cambridge citizens destroy university charters in riots

1332-1400 William Langley
John Wycliffe ✝ 1384

John of Gaunt ✝ 1399

1382 **Geoffrey Chaucer**; *"The Parliament of Fowls"*
1385 **Geoffrey Chaucer**, *"Troilus and Criseyde"*
1386 **Geoffrey Chaucer**, *"The Legend of Good Women"*
1387 **Geoffrey Chaucer**, *"Canterbury Tales"*

after 1381 **John Gower** *"Vox clamantis"* ("The History of the Peasants' Revolt.")
1380-84 Wycliffe arranges the translation of the Bible (reformative movement in Middle England)
1383 **Wycliffe** translates *New Testament* into English

1400	Henry IV ✟ 1413 Henry V	1420

1400 1401 1402 1403 1404 1405 1406 1407 1408 1409 1410 1411 1412 1413 1414 1415 1416 1417 1418 1419 1420

1400 Robert III ✟ 1406	James I	1420

Humanism

Henry IV, son of John of Gaunt and grandson of Edward III, married (1) Mary, daughter of Humphrey de Bohun(Earl of Hereford and Essex); (2) Joan, daughter of Charles II of Navarre. He died at Westminster, March 20, 1413.
Henry V, son of Henry IV, married Catherine, daughter of Charles VI of France; he died at Vincennes, Aug. 31, 1422.

1400
Richard II ✟ at Pontefract Castle

1406 King James of Scotland kidnapped at sea at the age of eleven
(He only returned to S. in 1424) ⇓

1406 Robert, duke of Albany **acted as Regent** during the captivity of James

Privilege of free speech in parliament   **1410 Three popes (Rome, Avignon, Milano)**
before 1413: no formal privilege of free speech   **1414   Equal rights for House of**
- speaker requested to be allowed to amend his report   **Commons**
- prayer that if the commons should say anything displeasing the king
  it should be forgiven, since the offence would not be intentionally regarded as customary
              Henry V revives claim to the French crown and **invades France** with10,000 men **1415**
              (Large parts of France (incl. Paris) occupied by the English)   ⇓

                    Battle of Agincourt won by the English   **1415**
                    Henry V is King of France

              Henry V takes James I with him to France. Scots fighting for   **1415**
              France were executed as they were in arms against their own
              King James I was then treated as an ally.

                    English conquest of Normandy: Murder of John of Burgundy **1419**
                              Treaty of Troyes with the French: Henry ∞ Katherine of Valois **1420**
       1403 Rebellion of the Percies (Earl of Northumberland and his son Hotspur)
                    allied with Owen Glendower. **Henry IV defeats them at Shrewsbury**

Architecture: Perpendicular Style (1375-1509

1400	⇒	**Welsh Rebellion**	⇒	**1409**	

1401 ⇒	⇒	⇒	⇒	⇒	⇒	**1414**
Prosecution of the Lollards (Followers of Wyclif´s belief)						**Lollard Complot**

       John Huss, Bohemian religious reformer influenced by Wycliffe **burnt at the stake**   **1415**
                                                            1415 Wycliffe banned as heretic

    English Population: In 1400 about 3,5 million people were living in the British Isles.

1400 The keep at *Warkworth Castle*, Northumberland, was built by the first Earl Percy.
It combined practical defence with elaborate living quarters and a beautiful, symmetrical
plan formed by overlaying a Greek cross with cauted edges on a similarly cauted square.
                                        1411 Foundation of the *University of St. Andrews*

LITERATURE
1400
Geoffrey Chaucer ✟ (poetry)
            1402
John Trevisa ✟ (most famous translator of the 14th cent.)

1400-1403 John Lydgate(1370-1449), *The Temple of Glass*
            1405/06 Thomas Hoccleve(1369-1437), *The male regle*
                        1411/12 Thomas Hoccleve(1369-1437),
                                The Regiment of Princes (5463 Lines)
                    John Lydgate (1370-1449) **completes** *The Troy Book* **1420**
                    Wyntonn, *The original Chronicle of Scotland* (Verse history)   **1420**
Morality Plays
1400 an., *The Pride of Life*
            1405 an., *The Castell of Perseverance*

1400 1401 1402 1403 1404 1405 1406 1407 1408 1409 1410 1411 1412 1413 1414 1415 1416 1417 1418 1419 1420

1420																				1440
1420	1421	1422	1423	1424	1425	1426	1427	1428	1429	1430	1431	1432	1433	1434	1435	1436	1437	1438	1439	1440
1420		1424					James I									1437			1440

Humanism

Henry VI, son of Henry V, born at Windsor 1421, married Margaret of Anjou, deposed March 1461, probably murdered in the Tower, 1471.
James I, (1394 - 1437), 18 years in Engl. custody, married Lady Jane Beaufort in 1424, crowned at Scone in 1424 and murdered at Perth in 1437, studied the works of Chaucer, and wrote The Kingis Quair.

1429 ●Jean d'Arc liberates Orleans
●Charles VII of France crowned
1431 Jean d'Arc burnt as a witch
1435 the English expelled
from France

Architecture: Perpendicular Style (1375-1509)

Manor Houses

Henry V

1422 ✶ William Caxton, first Engl. printer
1425 ✶Robert Henryson

Robert Henryson Robene and Makyne; The Testament of Cresseid, Morall Fabillis of Esope
1420 John Lydgate The Siege of Thebes   1430 The Falls of Princes
     1421 Thomas Hoccleve Hoccleve's Complaint
        1422 The Emperor Jereslaus' Wife; The Tale of Jonathas

1420	1421	1422	1423	1424	1425	1426	1427	1428	1429	1430	1431	1432	1433	1434	1435	1436	1437	1438	1439	1440

Humanism

**Window tracery
Lincoln Cathedral**

1445 Henry VI ¥ Margaret of Anjou
1449/50 French overrun Normandy
1450 Murder of the Duke of Suffolk (one of Henry´s confidentials) and John Cade´s rebellion (London seized and the King´s ministers denounced)
1453 ●French overrun Gascony (E. territories in S.W. France are lost except for Calais)
●End of Hundred Years War
●Henry VI becomes ill
1455 Beginning of the War of the Roses (House of Lancaster = Red Rose / House of York = White Rose)
1455 Battle of St.Albans (between Richard, duke of York, +. the Royalist Forces, Lancastrians)
Defeat of the Duke of York at Blore Heath +. Ludford Bridge**1459**

High Perpendicular Period (1375-1509) Main Features:

●vertical lines in window tracery ●wood and stone panelling ●fan-vault and flattened four-centred arch ●slenderness and delicacy in exterior silhouette ●detail of pinnacles and turrets●enlargement of window area
1441 Henry VI founds Eton, Buckinghamshire and King´s College,
1446 (-1515) Building of King´s College Chapel, Cambridge
1448/49 Queen´s College, Cambridge
1450 Great Chalfield Manor, Wiltshire
1445 Invention of book printing by Gutenberg (1400-1468)
1451(-1506)✱ Christoph Columbus
1455 Gutenberg prints the "42-Line" Bible at Mainz. First book printed with movable type

General structure: (engl. + scot. Chaucer-followers; (engl. + scot. Ballads of Tradition; (secular a. ecclesiastical Carols)
(Drama: Miracle-,Morality a. Mystery-Plays)
John Lydgate (poetry) **1449**
John Shirely (copies of Chaucer a. Lydgate) **1456**

1450 (anon.,Robin Hood and the Monk (First real ballad)
1450 (anon.,Cevy Chase (Border-Ballad)
1450 (anon.,I sing of a Maiden (Carol)

1450 (Reginald Pecock (1395-1460), The Repressor of Over Much Blaming of the Clergy
1451-1471 Thomas Malory(1393-1471), Le Morte Darthur

1450 (Wakefield Master The Townley Cycle (Mystery-Play)
1450 anon., Abraham and Isaac (Miracle Play)

England´s Wealth, Population & Social Structure in the 15th cent:

●**Peasants:** Their living-standard rose, they could even insist on higher wages + build stone houses! ●**Landowners:** They had to face some difficulties because market production in wheat + wool was less profitable, the cultivated area of E. was contracted + agricultural investments were curtailed. Moreover, wages + other costs rose. ●**Magnates and Gentry:** They drew their wealth out of different sources: 1.)Royal patronage 2.)Family inheritance 3.)Fortunate marriage 4.) They could gain money in the King´s or war service
●**Population**: in 1450 about 2,5 million people or less were living in E. and only from 1460 onwards did the population begin to rise at all. But the level of 1300 (4 million) wasn´t reached again until the 17th c.●**Trade:** Textile industry (wool), lead, tin, coal + iron-mining. Wine + sugar from Portugal to E. ●**Trade-Combinations**: emerged 1450 from which craftsmen could be expelled, if they didn´t obey the rules laid down by the wealthy men of their craft.

1460 1461	Henry VI	Edward IV	Henry VI	Edward IV 1480

1460	1461	1462	1463	1464	1465	1466	1467	1468	1469	1470	1471	1472	1473	1474	1475	1476	1477	1478	1479	1480

1460	James III	1480

Humanism

1460 Richard, duke of York, claims the Crown and dies at Wakefield

1461 Deposition of Henry VI + accession of Edward IV, Richard´s son

1465 Capture of Henry VI (Imprisoned in the Tower of London, while the Queen and their son seek shelter in France + Scotland)

1469 Rebellion of the earl of Warwick, the duke of Clarence, Lancastrians + dissident Yorkists against Edward IV

1470/71 Deposition of Edward IV + Return of Henry VI for one year. Edward escapes to Burgundy

1471 Edward IV returns to London + vanquishes Henry´s wife + son. Henry is probably killed in the Tower of London. Edward IV becomes King again.

1475 Edward IV undertakes an expedition to France, where E.´s allies Brittany and Burgundy turn out to be fickle. ⇓
1475 Treaty of Picquigny (Anglo-French treaty, where Louis XI provides Edward IV with a financial inducement to retire to England)

Wars of the Roses
The Battle of Nibley Green is the last fought between the private armies of feudal magnates.

Architecture: Perpendicular Style (1375-1509

1470 Needham Market Church (Perpendicular timber-roof)

1460 Ockwells Manor House, Bray

1475 Work on St George´s (Timber & brick used, original Chapel ,Windsor, began heraldic glas) (Flattened four-centred arch)
William Baker started work on the „Miracles of the Virgin" in **1479**, which are wall-paintings in Eton College

1465 ✳ Erasmus of Rotterdam

1473 ✳ Nikolaus Kopernikus
✳ Thomas More **1478**
1476 William Caxton (1422-91) founds printers in Westminster + prints Chaucer´s *Canterbury Tales*

1460 Sir Thomas Malory ✝ (prose) 1471
1460 Reginald Pecock ✝ (prose)
1464 John Capgraves ✝ (prose)

1476 John Fortescue ✝ (prose)

POETRY   **1465** Robert Henryson (1430-1506?),The Testament of Cresseid
1460 ✳ William Dunbar (✝ 1520 - poetry)   George Ashby ✝ (poetry) 1475

1475 ✳ Gavin Douglas (poetry)
1475 ✳ Stephen Hawes (poetry)

1475~anon.,The Flower and the Leaf
anon., Lancelot of the Lakes

Morality Plays   **1470**~ an.,Wisdom

1475~an.,Mankynde

1460	1461	1462	1463	1464	1465	1466	1467	1468	1469	1470	1471	1472	1473	1474	1475	1476	1477	1478	1479	1480

| 1480 | 1483 Edward V/Richard III 1485 | Henry VII 1500 |

| 1480 | 1481 | 1482 | 1483 | 1484 | 1485 | 1486 | 1487 | 1488 | 1489 | 1490 | 1491 | 1492 | 1493 | 1494 | 1495 | 1496 | 1497 | 1498 | 1499 | 1500 |

| 1480 | James III | 1488 | James IV | 1500 |

Humanism

Edward IV ☩   **1483** Succession of Edward V (minority)
1483 Murder of Edward V / Richard Duke of York in Tower of London
1483 Succession of Richard III - House of York
Richard III ☩   **1485**
1485 Battle of Bosworth Field - End of the Wars of the Roses
1485 Succession of Henry VII - House of Tudor
1485 Navigation Act (to support English seafarers and sea trade)

1486 Henry Tudor ¥ Elizabeth of York
1486 ❀ Prince Arthur
1486 Fellowship of the Merchant Adventurers formed
1487 Attempt to depose Henry VII through Lambert Simnel
1489❀Princess Margaret
1490 2nd Navigation Act

1491❀Prince Henry
1491-1497 Renewed attempts to depose Henry VII by
Perkin Warbeck; support from Ireland, Emperor
Maximillian, James IV of Scotland
1492 Peace with France (Henry renounces all rights to
French throne)
1494 Prince Henry named
Lord Lieutenant of Ireland
1495 Defacto Act of Parliament
(Amnesty for Yorkists who fought
against Henry in War of the Roses)
Intercursus Magnus **1496**
(Lifting of the trade embargo against the Netherlands)
1496❀Princess Mary
Ceasefire with Ireland **1497**
Perkin Warbeck hanged **1499**
1492 Columbus discovers America
Aberdeen University founded **1494**
John Cabot discovers Newfoundland **1497/8**

Richard III (2 October 1452 – 22 August 1485) was King of England and Lord of Ireland from 1483 until his death in 1485. He was the last king of the House of York and the last of the Plantagenet dynasty. His defeat and death at the Battle of Bosworth Field, the last decisive battle of the Wars of the Roses, marked the end of the Middle Ages in England.

Richard III ca 1520

Architecture: Late Perpendicular Style

Henry VII set about preserving the peace in England after years of political turmoil in which the Crown no longer held the upper hand against an over powerful aristocracy. - political stability was his main priority. He streamlined the old system of govt., altering the system of patronage and introducing capable advisors. The aristocracy became, throughout his reign, more subservient to the Crown, on his death it had become an apparatus necessary for the running of the country, but financially less cumbersome. By the end of Henry VII´s reign, the crown was more financially independent than it had been in previous decades.

One of the main developments in the early part of Henry´s reign was the growth in sheep-farming - supported by the growth of English exports of wool/wool products to the continent. This development in its turn led to an increase in enclosures by landlords - with the inevitable negative social consequences. Preventative measures were eventually taken **1489,** when the first **Acts against Enclosure** were introduced.

1484 ❀ William Tyndale
1490 ❀ Thomas Elyot
1490 ❀ David Lindsay
1497 ❀ John Heywood
1488 ❀ Miles Coverdale
1495 ❀ John Bale
1489 ❀ Thomas Cranmer
William Caxton☩ **1491**
Anon: A little Geste of Robin Hood (poetry) **1495**
John Skelton: Bowage of Court (Satire) **1498-99**
1489 John Skelton: On the Dolorous Death of the Duke of Northumberland
Henry Medwell: Fulgens & Lucrece (Secular Drama) **1497**
1484 W. Caxton translates Historyes and fables of Esope
Caxton prints:
1483 Confessio Amantis (Gower)
1484: Troilus and Criseyde (Chaucer)
1485 Le Morte Dartur (Malory)
1485 Sir Thomas Malory translates Le morte Dartur
1486 Henry Medwall The Play of Nature (morality)
1485 The Worlde and the Chylde

Renaissance

1501 ✳Anne Boleyn(2)
1501 Prince Arthur ∞ Catherine of Aragon
Prince Arthur✠1502
1503 Margaret Tudor ∞ James IV
1504 Henry VII deprives Common Law Court of power

1512 ✳Catherine Parr(6)
1512 War with Scotland and France
1513 Victory over Scotland at Flodden
1515 ✳Anne of Cleve(4)
1516 ✳Mary Tudor

Henry VII✠ 1509
1509 Henry VIII ∞ Catherine of Aragon (1)

Thomas Wolsey (Archbishop of York and 1517
Cardinal) gains several duties under Henry

Riots in London against undesirable aliens 1517

Wolsey becomes legate of the pope and makes a lot of changes to increase 1518
the crown's income. Wolsey and Henry aim to subordinate the church to
the crown.

Roots of the English reformation:
John Wycliffe proclaims the importance of the bible's priority over the rules of church. (He elaborates the first English translation of the
bible.)

Gothic takes its place in the "perpendicular style" (fan-shaped vaults, flat arches, perpendicular tracery). Together with influences of the
renaissance this forms the "Tudor style" (eg.: Hampton Court).

"Anti-clerical revolution":
The church has an exceptional position (no seat in the House of Commons) and therefore hardly any contact with the population. The
clergy functions as royal counsellor and is selected by the king. The possessory envy of common laymen leads to secularisation to the
crown`s profit. Financial and moral bankruptcy of the Church follows.

Architecture: Late Perpendicular Style -1509

1509 -14 Erasmus of Rotterdam in England

1512 Founding of St. Paul`s school
by John Colet
William Grocyn (lecturer in Oxford for Greek) ✠ 1519
1503 ✳ Sir Thomas Wyatt   1517 ✳ Henry Howard
1505 ✳ Nicholas Udall   Earl of Surrey
John Colet (✳January 1467) was an English churchman and educational pioneer. 16 September ✠ 1519
1515 ✳ Roger Ascham

(Interlude) 1503 John Skelton, Bowge of Court   1516 Magnificence
1507 Skelton, Phylyppe Sparowe
1509 Alexander Barcley, The Ship of Foolys of the Worlde (14.000 verses)
John Skelton, Colyn Clout (libellous pamphlet against Cardinal Wolsey) 1519

Erasmus of Rotterdam, Encomion morias seu laus stultiae 1511
(allegorical satire with drawings by H. Holbein)
Thomas Morus, Utopia II 1515
Erasmus of Rotterdam, "Novum Instrumentum 1516
(modern bible science)
Thomas Morus, Libellus vere aureus nec minus salutaris 1516
quam festivus de optimo reipublicae statu
de- que nova insula Utopia" (Utopia I)
Thomas Morus "Hystory of Kyng Rychard" 1516
Morality Play   1509 an., The Somonynge of Everyman

Renaissance

1521 ☀Catherine Howard (5)
1521 Henry VIII publication (Assertio Septem Sacramentorum)
   1522 ⇒ 1525 French-English War
       1525 Cardinal Wolsey >> Amicable Loan <<
        1526 England, France, Vatican City, Italy form an alliance against Charles V
         1527 Henry VIII insists on cancellation of the papal dispensation (marriage)
         1527 Henry and Catherine (divorce)
          1529 Thomas Morus Lord Chancellor
          1529 Breakdown of the policy of Wolsey
           1530 Incorporation of the English merchants in Spain
            1532 Thomas Cromwell Councillor: domestic reforms
            1532 Henry VIII prohibition of Acts of Annates
             1533 Henry VIII ∞ Anne Boleyn
             1533 Thomas Cramer Archbishop of Canterbury
             1533 ☀ Elisabeth, ✝1603
             1533 Dissolution of the Monasteries
              1534 Act of Supremacy Treason Act
              1534-1540 Geraldinische Liga Breakdown
          Thomas More ✝ **1536**
         Court of Augmention **1536** Royal Injunctions
         Catherine of Aragon ✝ **1536**
        Execution of Anne Boleyn ✝ **1536**
        Henry VIII ∞ Jane Seymour **1536**
      Pilgrimage of Grace Ten Articles **1536**
        Reconstruction of Navy **1536**
          ☀Eduard VI **1537**
           Six Articles **1539**

Deal Castle

Architecture: Tudor Style

Deal Castle is an artillery fort constructed by Henry VIII in Deal, Kent, between 1539 and 1540. It formed part of the King's Device programme to protect against invasion from France and the Holy Roman Empire and defended the strategically important Downs anchorage off the English coast. Comprising a keep with six inner and outer bastions, the moated stone castle covered 0.85 acres (0.34 ha) and had sixty-six firing positions for artillery. It cost the Crown a total of £27,092 to build the three castles of Deal, Sandown and Walmer, which lay adjacent to one another along the coast and were connected by earthwork defences.[a] The original invasion threat passed

              1532 J. Holbein (portrait of Henry VIII)
       John Skelton ✝ **1529**   William Tyndale ✝ **1536**
1520 ☀ Richard Puttenham **1525** ☀ Thomas Wilson

                    1536 ☀Thomas Sackville
            1532 ☀ Thomas Norton

1521 John Skelton, Speak, Parrot
 1522 John Skelton, Colin Clont
  1523 John Skelton, The Garland of Laurel

                   1536 John Skelton, King Johan
   1524 William Tyndale, Translation of the Testament
       1530 William Tyndale, Pentateuch
       1531 Thomas Elyot, The Boke named the Governour

        Thomas Elyot, Dictionary (lat. - engl.) **1538**
          Miles Coverdale, The Great Bible **1539**

1540	Henry VIII✝	1547	Edward VI	1553	Mary I	1558	1560

1540	1541	1542	1543	1544	1545	1546	1547	1548	1549	1550	1551	1552	1553	1554	1555	1556	1557	1558	1559	1560

1540 James V ✝ 1542	Mary, Queen of Scots	1560

Renaissance

1540 ✝ Thomas Cromwell (execution)
1540 Henry VIII ∞ Anne of Cleve
1540 Divorce from Anne of Cleve
1540 Henry VIII ∞ Catherine Howard
    1541 Henry becomes King of Ireland and head of the Irish Church
       1542 Catherine Howard executed
          1543 Henry VIII ∞ Catherine Parr
          1543 French War 1546
          1543 Ally with Emperor Charles V
          1543 - 1546 war against France, Scotland and European Catholics
                  1546 Establishment of Trinity College
                     1547 Thomas Seymour ∞ Catherine Parr
              Henry VIII ✝ **1547**
                    1547 Edward VI becomes king, but Edward Seymour,
                         Earl of Hereford, acts as regent during Edwards VI's minority.
                          1549 Fall of Seymour. John Dudley, Earl of Warwick regent
                          1549 First Book of Common Prayer
                             1550 Boulogne is returned to France
                             1552 2nd ed. of Book of Common Prayer

                                1553 Mary I Tudor, the Catholic **becomes Queen**, reintroduction of the Catholic Church in England.

Parliament repeals the Act of supremacy, **reinstates the heresy laws** and **1554** and petitions for reunion against the queen's catholic and Spanish policy

                                1554 Mary Tudor ∞ Philip of Spain
                                  1554 3000 men march on London .
                                  1554 1st share company is founded,
                                      the Muscovy Company.
                                      Anne of Cleve✝ **1557**
                            war with Spain against France **1557**
                                      Mary Tudor✝ **1558**
                                   Loss of Calais 1558
                                  3rd act of Uniformity **1559**

Architecture: Tudor Style

    1542 ✳ George Gascoigne
    1542 ✳ Sir Thomas Wyatt   Al Barday ✝ **1552**   **1556** ✳ Nicholas Udall
      1543 ✳ Thomas Deloney   **1552** ✳ Edmund Spenser
         1545 ✳ Nicholas Breton   **1554** ✳ John Lyly
      Thomas Elyot ✝ **1546**   **1554** ✳ Sir Philipp Sidney
  Henry Howard, Earl of Surrey ✝ **1547**   Thomas Cranmer ✝ **1556**
                                  Thomas Lodge ✳ **1558**

1540 **Howard Henry.** *Translation of Vergil's Äneis*
                            Tottel's Miscellany: Poetry and Lyrics (first English anthology) **1557**
             Henry Howard. *Songs and Sonnets*, (introduction of blank verse and the Italian Sonnet form) **1557**

         1545 **Roger Ascham.** *Toxophilus*
         1546 **John Heywood.** *A dialogue of Proverbs*
         1546 **Lyly/William/Odet** .*A short introduction to Grammar*
                  1551 **Robynson** .Translation of "Utopia" into English,
                  1552 **Hall.** *The Union of the Two Noble and Illustre Families of Lancaster and York,*
                        1553 **Wilson.** *Arte of Rhetorique*
              Thomas Sackville, ed. *A mirror for Magistrates* **1559**

                      1553 **Nicholas Udall.** *Ralph Roister Doister*
                1552 an. *Gammar Gurtons Nedle*   **1559**
                  Sackville/Norton, *A Mirror for Magistrates*

1540	1541	1542	1543	1544	1545	1546	1547	1548	1549	1550	1551	1552	1553	1554	1555	1556	1557	1558	1559	1560

Renaissance

1560 Elizabeth I forces Irish Parliament to accept "Common Prayer Book"
  1561 Mary Stuart returns from exile in France to Scotland
    1562 Beginning of English slave trade
      1563 Elizabethan Religious Settlement is completed with the **39 articles by the Archbishop of Canterbury**
        1564 Contract of Troyes, terminates Elizabeth's unsuccessful intervention in the French religious war
          1568-70 The French, Spaniards, the Irish, the Pope, and English Catholics want Mary Stuart (Queen of Scots) on the English throne
          1568 The Dutch war of independence against the Spaniards
            1570 "Regnants in excelsis", Pope Pius' V. bull excommunicates Queen Elizabeth
            1571 Several plots (Ridolfi plot, Norfolk plot etc.) to kill Queen Elizabeth and put Mary Stuart on the throne in order to recatholicize England
              1572 Many French Huguenots escape to England
          Sir Francis Drake's world circumnavigation **1577-80**

            1574 Queen Elizabeth issues a **royal patent** permitting the Earl of Leicester's players to play in London or any other city or

Queen Mary

            1576 J.Burbage (contemporary actor) **builds** the *first theatre in England,* called "The Theatre"
          The **playhouse** "*The Curtain*" opens. **1577**

1560 *Westminster School* is founded
    1565 First potato imports from South America
      1566 *Royal exchange* in London is founded
        1567 The "Bishop's Bible" is first official Bible in England

Architecture: Elizabethan Style

1560 ✳ Robert Green   George Gascoigne   ✝ 1577
  1561 ✳ Francis Bacon   Roger Ascham ✝ **1568**
    1562 ✳ Samuel Daniel   1570 ✳ Thomas Dekker
      1563 ✳ Michael Drayton   **1572** ✳ John Donne
        1564 ✳ William Shakespeare   **1572** ✳ Ben Jonson
        1564 ✳ Christopher Marlowe
          1567 ✳ Thomas Nashe

1560 The Genevan Bible
  1561 Hoby. Translation of Baldassare Castiglione´s *The Courtier*
    1562 Thomas Sackville (et al.) *"A Mirror for Magistrates*
      1568 The Bishop's Bible
        1570 (posthum) **Roger Aschan,** *"The Schoolmaster"*
  George Gascoigne, Certain Notes of Instruction concerning the making of verse **1575**
              John Lyly, *Anatomy of Wit* **1578**
            Edmund Spenser, *Shepherds' Calendar* **1579**

1560 1561 1562 1563 1564 1565 1566 1567 1568 1569 1570 1571 1572 1573 1574 1575 1576 1577 1578 1579 1580

1560 an, *Gammer Gurton's Needle* **1566 Gascoigne** *Supposes*   **1575** *The Classe of Government*
  1561 Thomas Norton / Thomas Sackville, *Gorboduc* or *Ferrex and Porrex*

1580 Mary, Queen of Scots ✝ (ex.)1587   James VI   **1600**

Renaissance

Mercantile Economy   *Body Politics* = Crown and Parliament form the basis of government
From approx. 1580 pauperismus = (process of impoverishment)   **1595 Irish Rebellion**
   1581 Establishment of Levonte Company   **1592 Plague in London**   against England
     1584 Private letters of marque are extended = Merchant Adventures   **1596 Hunger riots**
     1585 Elizabeth sends 6.000 soldiers under the Earl of Lancaster to main-
     tain the Protestant rebellion in Ireland   **1598 Poor laws 1598**
     1585 Elizabeth wages open **war on Philipp II of Spain**   Buildings of the Hanseatic League
     1585 Founding of the East India Company   are closed down in London
     1585 Establishment of the High Church within Anglicanism
     1585-1597 Spain at war against the rest of Europe   **1596-97 Further attacks**
     1587 England is at war with Spain   by **the Spanish**
   1582 Introduction of the   **1587 Execution of the Scottish Queen Mary Stuart**

    Gregorian calendar   **1587** Start of the **Armada Catholica**
     1588 Spanish **Armada is crushed**
     1588 Beginning of **England**'s rise to become a **leading maritime power**
   1583 Sir Humphrey **Gilbert discovers Newfoundland**
    1584 The **first English colony in North America** is founded by Sir Walter Raleigh.

1580✳Thomas Middleton   1588✳ Thomas Hobbes   Robert Southwell ✝ 1595   Edmund Spenser ✝ 1599
1580 ✝ Raphael Holinshed   Christopher Marlowe ✝ 1593
    Sir Philip Sidney ✝ 1586   Robert Greene   ✝ 1592   George Peele ✝ 1597

        Thomas Kyd   ✝ 1594

1580 Sir Philip Sidney, *Arcadia*   **1595** *Epithamalion*
   1581 *Astrophel and Stella*   **1586 Edmund Spenser,** *Astrophel*   **1596** books 4-6 of
     1589 *, The Fairy Queen* (books 1-3)   *The Fairy Queen*
1580 Sidney *Defence of Poesie*   **1588** *The History of Orlando Furioso*   **1596** *Four Hymns*
     1596 *Prothamalron*
    1592-98 William Shakespeare, *The Sonnets*
    1592-94 *Venus and Adonis* and *The Rape of Lucrece*
    1593-98 John Donne, *Satires*
1580 John Lyly, *Euphues and His England*   **1588** *Pandosto, or Dorastus and Fawnia*   **1595** *Colin Clout's* Come

    1591 *Endymion*   *Home Again*
    1592 *Galathea   Midas*
    1592   **1580 Sir Philip Sidney,** *The Defence of*
    1592 Greene, *A Quip for an Upstart*   Poesy
    1593 Hooker books 1-4, *Of the Laws of*
       Ecclesiastical Polity
     1597 Book 5
   Francis Bacon, *First Ten Essays*   **1597**
1587-88 Christopher Marlowe, *Tamburlaine the Great*
   1588-92 *Doctor Faustus*   **1593** *Edward the Second*   **1598**
    1590 *The Jew of Malta*   **Ben Johnson**, *Every*
     1592 *The Massacre at Paris*   *Man in His Humour*
   1589-91 Robert Greene *Friar Bacon and Friar Bungay*
    1590 William Shakespeare, *1-3 Henry VI*
    1590-94 *The Comedy of Errors*   **1596/97-98** *Henry IV*
    1590-98 *The two Gentlemen of Verona*   **1598**
     1592/93 *Richard III*   *As You Like It*
    1591 *King John*   **1598** *Much*
Elizabeth I   **1591-97/98** *Romeo and Juliet*   *Ado about Nothing*
  1588 *The History of Orlando Furioso*
    1593-95 *Love Labour's Lost*   **1598**
   1589 *The Taming of the Shrew*   *The Merry Wives of Windsor*
   1589-90 *Titus Andronicus*   **1594** *The Merchant of Venice*
   1589 Thomas Kyd   *Pompey*   **1594** *A Midsummer-Night's Dream*
    the Great   *Solyman and Perseda*   *The Spanish Tragedy*
     1594-97/98 *Richard II*   **1599**
     Henry V   *Julius Caesar Hamlet*
   1591-94 George Peele. *The Old Wives' Tale*
    1593 Thomas Heywood. *Fast Bind, Fast Find*

Renaissance

1600 Foundation of the **East India Company**

    1601 Essex's rebellion

Elizabeth✝ **1603** Accession of **James VI of Scotland as James I**;
    Peace in Ireland; Millenary Petition of the Puritans

    1604 Peace with Spain (**treaty of London**);
    Hampton Court Conference (King, Bishops and Puritans)

    1605 Gunpowder Plot fails (last major Catholic conspiracy)

    1606-1607 Failure of James's plans for union of kingdoms

    1607 First permanent settlement of Virginia

    1609 Rebellion of the Northern Earls in Ireland;
    beginnings of the Planting of Ulster
    by Scots and English protestants

    1610 Failure of Great Contract (Reform of royal finance)

Prince Henry ✝**1612**

    1613 Princess Elizabeth ✝ Elector Palatine
Ascendancy of **George Villier** Duke of Buckingham **1617-1629**

The Pilgrim Fathers inaugurate religious migration to New England

1600 4 million inhabitants   **1619-1622**
    4/5 of the population works in agriculture   **Inigo Jones** (1572-1651)
    designs the *Banqueting House*,

Architecture: Jacobean Style

    1611 Publication of *Authorised Version of the Bible*
    (Anglican and Puritan co-operation)

John Lyly✝ **1606**

✝ **1601** Thomas Nashe   **1606** ✳ Sir William D'Avenant

    1605 Francis Bacon *The Advancement of Learning*   **Thomas Hobbes**

metaphysical poetry

John Donne George Herbert   **Richard Crashaw**   **James Shirley**   **Andrew Marvell**   **Henry Vaughan**   **Thomas Traherne**

1600 1601 1602 1603 1604 1605 1606 1607 1608 1609 1610 1611 1612 1613 1614 1615 1616 1617 1618 1619 1620

1601 ✳ John Earle   **1608** ✳John Milton   **William Shakespeare** ✝ **1616**   **1618** ✳

    1605 ✳Thomas Browne   **1613** ✳Richard Crashaw Abraham Cowley

John Lyly ✝ **1606**   **1612** ✳Samuel Butler

    1618 John Seldon
    History of Tithes

    1611 Donne *An Anatomy of the World*

1600 Ben Jonson *The Fountain of Self-Love*   **1613** Ben Jonson *Bartholomew Fair*

    1601 Ben Jonson *The Poetaster***1606** *Volpone or the Fox***1610** Ben Jonson *The Alchemist*   **1616** *The Devil is an Ass*

    1603 *Jonson Sejanus His Fall*   **1611** Shakespeare *The Tempest*

1600 Thomas Dekker *The Shoemaker's Holiday*   **1609** Ben Jonson *Epicoene, or The Silent Woman*

1600 Shakespeare *Henry V*   **1606** Dekker *A Yorkshire Tragedy*

    1604 Dekker/Middleton *The Honest Whore* **1611** John Ford *A King And No King*   Chapman   **1619**

    1601 Shakespeare *Julius Caesar*   **1607** Shakespeare *Antony and Cleopatra*   *The Humorous Lieutenant*

1600 Chapman *May Day* **1604** Shakespeare *Othello, the Moor of Venice*   **1612** John Webster *The White Devil*

1600 Shakespeare *Twelfth Night, or: What you Will* **1608** Shakespeare *Coriolanus*

    1601 Shakespeare *All's Well that Ends Well*   **1608** Shakespeare *Pericles* **1613** Webster *The Duchess of Malfi*

    1607 Shakespeare *Timon of Athens*

    1602 Shakespeare *Hamlet* **1606** Shakespeare *Macbeth* **1611** Beaumont/Fletcher *A King and No King*

    1603 Shakespeare *Measure for Measure*   **1610** Shakespeare *The Winter's Tale*

    1603 Shakespeare *Troilus and Cressida***1609** Shakespeare *Cymbeline*

    1607 Chapman *Bussy D'Ambois*   **1613** Chapman The Revenge of Bussy D'Ambois

    1604 John Marston *The Malcontent*   **1611** Beaumont/Fletcher *Cupid's Revenge*

    1601 Chapman *All Fools* **1605** Shakespeare *King Lear* **1610** John Fletcher *The Faithful Shepherdess*

    1601 Marston *What you Will***1605** Thomas Middleton *A Trick to Catch the Old One*

    1605 Chapman *Monsieur d'Olive* **1607** Thomas Heywood *A Woman Killed with Kindness*

1600 Dekker *The Pleasant Comedy of Old Fortunatus* **1608** Beaumont/Fletcher *Four Plays in One*

1600 Heywood *The Four Prentices of London* **1607** Cyril Tourneur *The Revenger's Tragedy*

    1602 Chapman *The Conspiracy and Tragedy of Charles Duke of Byron*

    1603 Dekker *Patient Grissill*

1622-1623 Charles I and Buckingham go to Spain
1624-1630 War with Spain
James I ✝ **1625** Accession of **Charles I**
and marriage to Henrietta Maria, sister of Louis XIII of France; Act of Revocation
1626-1629 War with France
1628 Petition of Right (taxation right of the
Parliament); assassination of Buckingham
1629-1640 Personal rule of Charles I, who dissolves Parliament,
determined to govern without
1621 Bacon accused of bribery by James I   **1630** large-scale emigration to Massachusetts begins (Puritan
1629-1632 economic depressions   persecution)

1633 William Laud translated to be
Archbishop of Canterbury
1634-1640 Ship Money Case
1637
John Hampden's case supports
Charles I's claims to collect Ship
Money

1637-1640 Breakdown
of Charles's government
of Scotland and two attempts
to impose his will by force

The House of Commons
(Engraving of 1624)

1634 1/4 of the population are
Catholics

1628 Publication of **Harvey**'s work on the circulation of the blood
Francis Bacon ✝ **1626**   **1631** ✳ John Dryden   **1635** ✳George Etherege
1625 John Fletcher ✝   Thomas Dekker ✝1632   **Sir Henry Wotton** ✝1639
Nicholas Breton ✝ **1626**   J   ohn Donne ✝ **1631**   Ben Jonson ✝ **1637**
Lancelot Andrewes ✝ **1626**   **1628**✳ John Bunyan   **1632** ✳ John Locke   Thomas Carew ✝1639
Thomas Middleton ✝ **1627**   John Webster ✝ **1634**
Cyril Tourneur ✝ **1626**   George Chapman ✝1634
John Fletcher ✝ **1625**   John Marston ✝ **1634**
1627 *Sylva Sylvarum* (publ.)   **1632** Donne J. *Death's Duel* (publ.)
1620 Bacon *Novum Organum Scientarum*   **1626** *The New Atlantis*   **1633 Edmund Spenser** *A View of the Present*
1622 *Historia Naturalis et Experimentalis*   **1628**John Earle *Micro-Cosmographie*   *State of Ireland* (publ.)
1622 Henry Peacham *The Complete Gentleman*
1625 *Apophthegms New and Old* 1   **1639**
1621 Robert Burton *The Anatomy of Melancholy*   **Thomas**Fuller *History of the Holy War*
1621 Joseph Hall *Works***1625 Samuel Purchas** *Hakluytes posthumus* **1632 John Milton***Lycidas; L'Allegro;Il Penseroso*
1624 John Donne *Devotions upon Emergent Occasions*   **1635 John Selden***Mare Clausum*
1621 *The Wild Goose Chase*   **1626** *Five Sermons*
1620 Thomas Dekker *The Virgin Martyr*   **1628** *Britannia Honour* **1632 James Shirley** *Hyde Park*
1621 *The Witch of Edmonton*   **1626** *The Noble Spanish Soldier*
1620 John Fletcher *The False One*   **1628 John Earle***Microcosmography*
1621 *The Wild GooseChase*   **1626 Ben Jonson** *The Staple of News* **1632** *Jonson The Magnetic Lady*
1624 John Fletcher *A Wife for a Month*   **1631 Thomas Heywood** *The Fair Maid of the West*
1620 Ben Jonson *News From the New World*   **1629-33 John Ford***Tis Pity She's a Whore*
1623 *Time Vindicated to Himself*   **1633 Thomas Heywood** *The English*
1621 Philip Massinger *The Duke of Milan*   *Traveller*
1622 *The Changeling***1625-27** *Women Beware Women*   **1634** D'Avenant *Love and Honour*

1640	Charles I ✝(ex.) 1649		1660

1640 1641 1642 1643 1644 1645 1646 1647 1648 1649 1650 1651 1652 1653 1654 1655 1656 1657 1658 1659 1660

1642	Civil War	1649	Commonwealth	1660

1653-1658 Oliver Cromwell Lord Protector

1640-1660 Long Parliament
1641 Remodelling of government in England and Scotland; Rebellion of Ulster Catholics
1642 King's attempt on the Five Members; his withdrawal from London; the 19 Propositions
1642-1649 Civil Wars ('Cavaliers' against 'Roundheads')
1643 King's armies prosper; the Scots invade England on the side of Parliament
1644 Parliamentary armies prosper, especially in the decisive battle of the war (Marston Moor)
1645 'Clubmen' risings of armed neutrals threaten both sides
1646 King surrenders to the Scots; Presbyterian Church established

John Pym ✝1643 **1647** ●Army revolt „Heads of the Proposal"
●radical movements criticize parliamentary tyranny
1641 Lord Strafford's Trial ●King prevaricates
1648 ●**Second Civil War:**
●Scots now side with the King and are defeated.
●Provincial risings crushed (Kent,Colchester...)
1649 Execution of Charles I
1649-1660 England a Republic
1649-1653 England governed by 'Rump' Parliament (Commonwealth)
Period of religious toleration, particularly for Puritans under O. Cromwell
1649-1650 Oliver Cromwell conquers Ireland (Drogheda massacre)
1650-1652 Cromwell conquers Scotland
(battles of Dunbar and Worcester)
1651 Navigation Act (import of English goods only
by English ships)
1652-54 First Dutch War
1655-1660 War with Spain
Oliver Cromwell ✝ **1658**
Richard Cromwell Lord Protector **1658-1659**
Richard Cromwell overthrown by the army; 'Rump' Parliament restored **1659**

Architecture: Stuart Style

✝ **1641** Thomas Heywood
✝ **1641** Thomas Dekker
1640 ✳ Mrs Aphra Behn **1650** ✳ Jeremy Collier
1641 ✳ William Wicherly **1652** ✳ Thomas Otway
1640 ✝John Ford Richard Crashaw ✝ **1649** **1653** ✳ Nathaniel Lee
1642 ✳ Thomas Shadwell **1647** ✳ John Wilmot John Hales ✝ **1656**
Sir John Suckling ✝ **1642** **1648** ✳ John Sheffield
Francis Quarles ✝ **1644** John Webster ✝ **1652**
1651 Thomas Hobbes *Leviathan* *of Troy* (transl.)
1656 Denham *The Destruction*

John Donne(✝1631)
1640 *Sermons* (Published) **1646** *Sermons*

1642 Denham *Cooper's Hill* **1647** Cudworth *Sermon preached before the House of Commons*
1644 John Milton *Areopagitica* **1649** *Tenure of Kings and Magistrates*
1643 John Milton *Doctrine and discipline of divorce* **1652** Herbert *A Priest to the Temple*
1646 *Steps to the Temple* **1651** Milton *Pro Populo Anglicano Defensio*
1644 Milton *On Education* **1655** Hobbes *De corpore*
1651 Hobbes Leviathan **1658** Hobbes
1645 Herbert *De religione gentilum* *De homine*
1647 Cowley *The Mistress* **1656** Cowley *Davideis*
1640 Carew *Poems* **1645** Waller *Poems* **1648** Herrick *Hersperides* **1656** Cowley *Miscellaneous Poems*
1649 Lovelace *Lucasta: Epodes, Odes, Sonnets, Songs*
1646 Vaughan *Poems, with the 10th Satire of Juvenal English*
1651 Vaughan *Olor Iscanus*
1650 Vaughan *Silex Scintillans*
1652 Vaughan *The Mount of Olives*
1654 Vaughan *Flores Solitudinis*
1642 Denham *The Sophy* **1656** D'Avenant *The Siege*
1640 Shirley *The Constand Maid* **1653** Rowley *The Spanish Gipsy of Rhodes*
1641 Shirley *The Cardinal* (Opera)

1640 1641 1642 1643 1644 1645 1646 1647 1648 1649 1650 1651 1652 1653 1654 1655 1656 1657 1658 1659 1660

1660 1661 1662 1663 1664 1665 1666 1667 1668 1669 1670 1671 1672 1673 1674 1675 1676 1677 1678 1679 1680

1660 Restoration

1660 Restauration of the Stuarts: Charles II King of England
1661-1664 Clarendon Code (Laws to establish the predominance of the Anglican Church)
1662 Church of England restored
1665-1667 Second Dutch War
1672-1674 Third Dutch War
1673 Test Act (civil servants have to be members of the Church of England)
Titus Oates reveals the Popish Plot intending the assassination of Charles II **1678**
Habeas Corpus Act (Law against violations of personal liberty) **1679**
Exclusion Crisis; political parties (Whigs and Tories) emerge **1679-81**

1660 Foundation of Royal Society (England's oldest academy of science)
1665 The Great Plague
1666 Great Fire of London
1668 William Penn (Quaker) committed to the Tower of London
1674 Grain bounties introduced (England self-sufficient in food)
1675-1710 Sir Christopher Wren (1632-1723) designs St Pauls Cathedral
1665 Samuel Pepys surveyor general of victualling office

Charles II

The Great Fire of London, depicted by an unknown painter (1675), as it would have appeared from a boat in the vicinity of Tower Wharf on the evening of Tuesday, 4 September 1666. To the left is London Bridge; to the right, the Tower of London. Old St Paul's Cathedral is in the distance, surrounded by the tallest flames.

Abraham Cowley ✝ **1667**
1667 ☀ Jonathan Swift
Sir William D'Avenant ✝ **1668**
1670 ☀ William Congreve
1672 ☀ Sir Richard Steele
1672 ☀ Joseph Addison
1674 ☀ Nicholas Rowe
1671 ☀ Colley Cibber

1660 Sermons (Published)
1669 William Penn No Cross, no Crown
1668 Sir William Temple Essay upon the present state of Ireland
Samuel Butler **1663-1678** Hudibras
John Milton   **1667** Paradise Lost   **1671** Paradise Regained
John Dryden   Mac Flecknoe **1678**
John Bunyan   **1666** Grace Abounding   The Pilgrim's Progress **1678**
1664 Dryden The Indian Queen   **1672** Mariage-à-la-Mode/All for Love **1678**
1664 Dryden The Rival Ladies   **1672** Wycherley The Gentleman Dancing-Master
1667 Dryden Secret Love   **1675** Wycherley The Country Wife

1660 1661 1662 1663 1664 1665 1666 1667 1668 1669 1670 1671 1672 1673 1674 1675 1676 1677 1678 1679 1680

1680 1681 1682 1683 1684 1685 1686 1687 1688 1689 1690 1691 1692 1693 1694 1695 1696 1697 1698 1699 1700

1683 Rye House Plot, Whigs proscribed

Charles II ✝ **1685** Failure of the rebellion by Charles's Protestant bastard son, James, Duke of Monmouth

1685 Accession of James II

1687 Declaration of Indulgence; Tories proscribed

1688 ●William of Orange invades
●James II takes flight

1688 ✳James's son James Francis Edward (The Old Pretender)
Glorious Revolution

1689 Accession of William III (of Orange) and Mary II

1689 Bill of Rights; Toleration Act (Rights for Trinitarian
Protestant dissenters)

1690 Battle of the Boyne (William III defeats Irish and French army)

Queen Mary ✝ **1694** Triennial Act (maximum duration
of Parliament: three years)

Civil List Act (maintenance of the royal household) **1697**

Inhabitants England & Wales

England & Wales 5.5 Mio

Scotland   1.5 Mio

Ireland   2   Mio

London   500.000

all other towns 850.000

E C O N O M I C S   1690 William Petty. Political Arithmetick

1694 Foundation of The Bank of England

Social structure **1688**	total no	income per head
Temporal Lords	6400	70
Spiritual Lords	520	65
Barons	12800	55
Knights	7800	50
Esquires	30000	45
Gentlemen	96000	35
Civil Servants	70000	25
Merchants	64000	37
Lawyers	70000	20
Clergy	52000	9
Landlords	980000	11
Peasants	750000	8
Artists	80000	12
Shopkeepers	180000	10
Artisans	240000	10
Officers	36000	18
Sailors	150000	7
Labourers/Servants	1275000	4
Paupers	1300000	2
Soldiers	70000	7
Vagrants/Beggars	30000	2

James II

Edmund Waller ✝ **1687**   **1689** ✳ Samuel Richardson

1680 ✝ Samuel Butler   John Bunyan ✝ **1688** Nathaniel Lee ✝ **1692**   Sir William Temple ✝ **1699**

1683 ✳ Edward Young   Thomas Shadwell ✝ **1692** Henry Vaughan ✝ **1695**

Thomas Otway ✝   **1685**   George Etheredge ✝ **1690**   **1692** ✳ Bishop Joseph Butler

Isaac Walton ✝ **1683**   Aphra Behn ✝ **1689**

1687 Isaac Newton Principia Mathematica   **1699** ✳ John Dyer

1685 John Locke Letters for Toleration   **1695** Locke The Reasonableness of Christianity

1685 ✳ John Gay   **1690** Locke An Essay Concerning Human Understanding

1690 Locke Two Treatises of Government

1685 Dryden Threnodia Augustalis   **1694-97** transl. of Aeneid 1699 Fables

1688 ✳ Alexander Pope

1680 John Bunyan *The Life and Death of Mr Badman*   **1693** Dryden *A Discourse concerning the Original*

1680 Sir William Temple *Miscellanea*   *and Progress of Satire*

1681 *Absalom And Achitophel*   **1687** *The Hind and the Panther*   **1697** *Alexander's Feast*

1682 Religio Laici; *The Medall; MacFlecknoe*

1680 Dryden *The Spanish Friar* **1685** *Albion and Albanius (Opera)*   **1693** *Love Triumphant*

1682 *The Duke of Guise* (with Nathaniel Lee**)**   **1691** *King Arthur (Opera)*

1690 Dryden *Amphitryon*

William Congreve   **1687 Sir Charles Sedley** *Bellamira*   **1693** *The Double Dealer; The Old Bachelor*

1695 *Love for Love*

1680 Mrs Aphra Behn *The Rover (II*)   **1688 Thomas Shadwell** *The Squire of Alsatia*   **1698 G.Farquhar**

1682 Thomas Shadwell *The Lancashire Witches* **1689** *Bury Fair*   *Love in a Bottle*

1680 Nath. Lee *Cesar Brogia; Theodosius, or The Force of Love*   **1699**

1682 Thomas Southerne *The Loyal Brother; The Persian Prince*   *The Constant Couple*

1684 Thomas Southerne *The Fatal Marriage Loyal Brother; The Persian Prince*

1682 Th. Otway *Venice Preserved*

1680 1681 1682 1683 1684 1685 1686 1687 1688 1689 1690 1691 1692 1693 1694 1695 1696 1697 1698 1699 1700

1700 William III ✝ 1702 Anne										1714		George I					1720

1700 1701 1702 1703 1704 1705 1706 1707 1708 1709 1710 1711 1712 1713 1714 1715 1716 1717 1718 1719 1720

1702 Tory	1704 Whig Government	1710 Tory Government 1714 Whig Government

(Harley, Bolingbroke) ⇒ **1716 Exile** in France

1701 ●Act of Settlement (⇒regulation
of Protestant inheritance;
monarchs have to be Anglican)

1711 Occasional Conforming Act
Foundation of the South Sea
Company

1717 Triple Alliance to preserve

James II ✝ ● in French exile

1702 ●Declaration of War against France
●War of Spanish Succession ⇒ ⇒ ⇒
●William III ✝

1713 Peace of Utrecht ✍
1713 End of Spanish Succession War
1715 Riot Act

1704 English Conquest of Gibraltar

Louis XIV ✝1715

1705 Newcomen's Steam Engine

1716 Septennial Act
length of Parliament 7 years.

1707 End of French War
1707 Act of Union
(with Scotland)

1715 Scottish Revolt in
favour of the Stuarts
dejected 1719

1700-1710 (1) Enclosure Act	1710-1720 (10) Enclosure Acts

1702 Buckingham Palace
1709 ●A. Darby begins **smelting iron in a coke** fire
●Production of large quantities of iron becomes
basis for rapid **growth of heavy industry**

1712 G.F.Händel in London

1711 Anthony A Cooper, Third Earl of Shaftesbury
Characteristicks of Men, Manners, Opinions, Times.
1713 A. Collins, *A Discourse of Free-thinking*
1714 B. de Mandeville (1670-1733)
The Fable of the Bees

1700 1701 1702 1703 1704 1705 1706 1707 1708 1709 1710 1711 1712 1713 1714 1715 1716 1717 1718 1719 1720

1700 ✝ John Dryden
Samuel Pepys ✝1703 George Farquhar✝1707
Anthony Ashley Cooper, Third Earl of Shaftesbury ✝ 1713

1709 ✳ Dr. Samuel Johnson

1717✳ D. Garrick
Nicholas Rowe ✝ 1718
Joseph Addison ✝ 1719

1700 ✳ James Thomson
1701 ✝ Sir Charles Sedley
Charles Sackville ✝ 1706
1703 ✳ John Wesley

1707 ✳ Henry Fielding 1711✳ David Hume
1713 ✳ Laurence Sterne 1717 ✳ Horace
William Wycherley ✝1715

1716 ✳ Thomas Gray
Walpole
Joseph Addison ✝1719

John Locke ✝1704 Natural Law: 'Society is natural and best when left alone.'

Weeklies: Steele/Addison/ 1709 Tatler 1711 Spectator 1712 1713 The Guardian

Architecture: Neo-Classicism

1700 1701 1702 1703 1704 1705 1706 1707 1708 1709 1710 1711 1712 1713 1714 1715 1716 1717 1718 1719 1720

1701 Daniel Defoe,*True-Born Englishman*
1704 Jonathan Swift, *The Tale of a Tub*

1709 *History of the Union of Great Britain*

1719
Robinson Crusoe

1712 *Proposal for Correcting the English*
Tongue
1711 Alexander Pope, *Essay on Criticism*
1712 *The Rape of the Lock; Windsor Forest*
1713 Joseph Addison *Cato*
1713 John Gay *Rural Sports* 1719
Young *Paraphrase on Part of the Book of Job*

1700 Congreve *The Way of the World*
1701 *The Judgement of Paris*
1702 Farquhar *The Twin Rivals* **1707** *The Beaux' Stratagem* **1712 Philips** *The Distrest Mother*
1705 Cibber *The Careless Husband*
1700 Nicholas Rowe *The Ambitious Stepmother* **1707 Cibber** *The Lady's Last Stake* **1714** *The Tragedy of Jane Shore*
1702 *Tamerlane*
1703 *The Fair Penitent*
1701 Steele *The Funeral* **1705** *The Tender Husband*
1703 *The Lying Lover*

1715 *The Tragedy of*
Jane Grey

1700 1701 1702 1703 1704 1705 1706 1707 1708 1709 1710 1711 1712 1713 1714 1715 1716 1717 1718 1719 1720

Wig Government

War against Spain **1739**

1721 Walpole in the position of the first **Prime Minister**
1726 War against Spain
1723 Bolingbroke returns from French Exile
1732 Downing Street became residence of
the **British prime minister**
1731/32 Prohibition of emigration to
1727 Gibraltar was besieged   America for workers in English
1729 Peace of **Seville**   manufacturing and factories
1730 Methodist Society
British-Russian trade contract which granted great advantages for English merchants **1734**
●**Porteous Riots** (=**lynch justice** against an officer in Edinburgh)**1736**
●**"Leicester House"** became the centre of the **Whig opposition**
1728 E. Chambers, *Cyclopaediaor Univ*

●**Queen Caroline✝ 1737**

1730 M.Tindal(1653-1733),

The Age of Landscape Gardening

1733 The invention of the **flying shuttle** for the
handloom strongly increased **weaving out-
put**

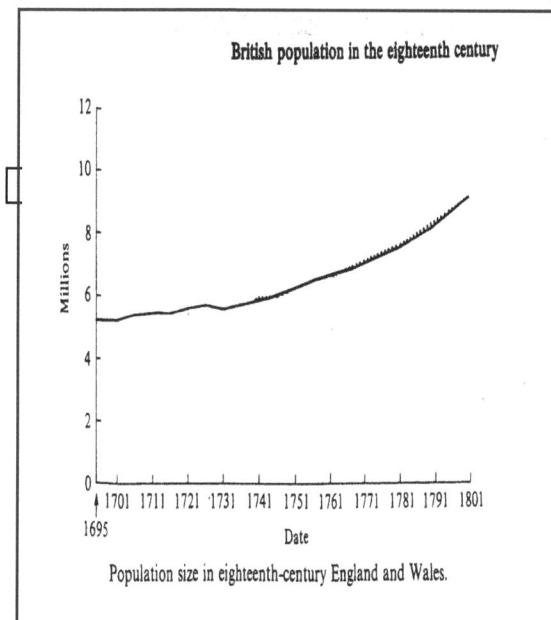

British population in the eighteenth century

Population size in eighteenth-century England and Wales.

J.Butler(1692-1752),   **1736**
fighter; against **deism**.
*The analogy of religion, natural and revealed,
to the constitution and course of nature*
W.Warburton(1698-1779),
represented the **Anglican church**   **1736**
The alliance between church and state; against **deism**,
Stage Licensing Act (=literary **1737**
censorship of the Anglican church)
Methodist movement was founded (represented deism)   **1738**

1723 ✳ Adam Smith

1721 ✝ Matthew Prior **✝**
Marlborough**✝1722**   Newton **✝ 1726**
1722 ✳Samuel Foote
1721 ✳ Tobias Smollett
John Toland **✝1722**

Matthew Tindal **✝ 1733**   ✳Georg III **1738**
Daniel Defoe **✝ 1731**   Macpherson
Richard Steele **✝ 1729** John Gay **✝ 1732**   **1736** ✳ James
1728 ✳Oliver Goldsmith,   George Lillo **✝ 1739**
William Congreve **✝ 1729**   **1731** ✳ William Cowper
Antony Collins   **✝ 1729**

1721 Alexander Pope, *To Mr. Addison*   **1731-35***Moral Essey I-IV*
1725/26 *Odyssey I-III*   **1733** *Essay on Man*
1728/9 *Dunicad I-IV*
1723 Matthew Prior, *Down Hall*   Bernard Mandeville **✝ 1733**
1727 John Gay, *Fables I*   *Fables II* **1738**
1728 *The Beggar's Opera*
1726-30 James Thomson, *The Seasons*   **1735/6** *Liberty I-V*

1729 *Britannia*
William Shenstone, *The Schoolmistress* **1736**
1725 John Dyer *Grongar Hill*   *Elegies on Several Occasions* **1737**
1725 Edward Young, *Universal Passion I-IV*
1728, *Ocean*
1726 Jonathan Swift, *Cadenus, and Vanessa*
1722 Daniel Defoe, *Plague Year, History of Peter the Great, Moll Flanders, Colonel Jack*
1725 *Jonathan Wild* **1728** *Captain Carleton*
1726 *History of the Devil*
1721 Jonathan Swift, *Holy Orders, Letter of Advice to a Young Poet*   **1735/7 Alexander Pope**, *Letters*
1726 *Gulliver's Travels*   **1735** *Collected Works*
1729 *Modest Proposal* **1733** *Life and Genuine Character of Dr.Swift*
1721 Edward Young, *The Revenge*   **1731 Lillo***The London Merchant*
1730 Henry Fielding, *Tom Thumb, Rape upon Rape*
1731 *The Letter Writers*   **1736** *Pasquin*
1732 *Modem Husband*
1733 *Don Quichote in England*

1740	1741	1742	1743	1744	1745	1746	1747	1748	1749	1750	1751	1752	1753	1754	1755	1756	1757	1758	1759	1760

1742 Majority of the Tories with a mixed cabinet of nearly all political parties in the Commons; Prime Minister: Henry Pelham

1740 War of Austrian Succession was opened on the continent
1741 A vote of confidence against **Walpole** failed
1742 ●**Walpole** lost nearly all of his **political power** and resigned;
●**England** conquered **French** colonies in America and India
1743 George II beat the French near Dettingen / Main
1744-45 Anglo-French sea war
1745 ●**Stuart followers** under Charles Edward were beaten near Prestonpans (Scotland);
●Dissolution of the Scottish clan-constitution

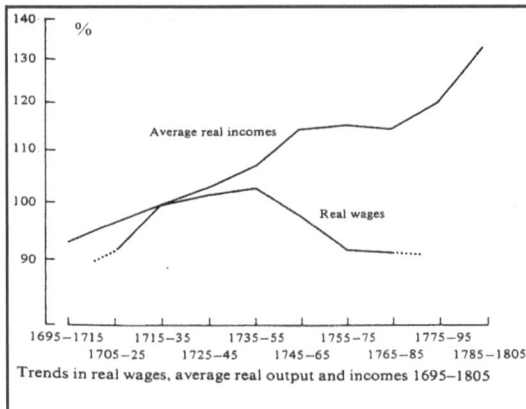
Trends in real wages, average real output and incomes 1695–1805

1748 Treaty of Aix-la-Chapelle ended the War of Austrian Succession
1751 in a border agreement the **French** gain **Montreal**
1756 (-1763) Seven Years War
with France, Austria and Russia on the side of Frederick the Great of Prussia.

This **Colonial War** was waged on three continents (Europe, America, Asia/India) and ended with British victories over France in India (Robert Clive, battle of Plassey 1757) and Canada (Wolfe captures Quebec in 1759), War ended by the **Treaty of Paris**.

William Pitt (Pitt the Elder 1708-78, Whig) became Minister of War. He began exercising **unrestricted control** in national and military affairs and directed the war on three continents on land and sea, but **lost power** on the succession of **George III**, who favoured the Tories. **1757/58**

Militia Bill; Pitt had organized military service and had founded the **Scottish Highland regiments** besides the regular army

1740	1741	1742	1743	1744	1745	1746	1747	1748	1749	1750	1751	1752	1753	1754	1755	1756	1757	1758	1759	1760

E C O N O M I C S   James Cantillion. Essay on the Nature of Commerce in General **1755**   **1758**
Francois Quesnay. Tableau Economique (Paris)
Adam Smith. *Theory of Moral Sentiments* **1759**

1740 First spinning machine factory opens in England (change from cottage textile industry to factory production)
1747 Bradley discovers the swaying of the earth' axis
1752 Calendar reform to the Gregorian system
1741/42 D. Hume (1711-1776),*Essays, Moral and Political*
1744 G. Berkeley(1685-1753), *Philosophical Reflections Concerning Tar-Water*
1748 D. Hume, *Enquiry Concerning Human Understanding*

Thomas Southerne ✝ **1746**   Henry Fielding ✝ **1754**   **1757** ✻ William Blake
Francis Hutcheson ✝**1746**   Joseph Butler **1752**   Edward Moore ✝ **1757**
Alexander Pope ✝ **1744**   **1748** ✻ Jeremy Bentham   Colley Cibber ✝ **1757**   W. Collins ✝
James Thomson ✝ **1748**   **1752** ✻ Thomas Chatterton   **1759**
1750 ✻ Robert Fergusson   John Dyer ✝**1757**   ✻ Robert Burns
1754 ✻ G. Crabbe

1742-45 Edward Young, *The Complaint*   **1755** *Centaur not Fabulous*
1748 Thomson *The Castle of Indolence*   Conjectures 1759
1750 Thomas Gray, *An Elergy Written in a Country Churchyard*

1749 Dr. Samuel Johnson, *Irene*
1753 Edward Moore, *Gil Blas*
The Gamester

1740 Colley Cibber, *Apology for the life of Mr. Cibber, Comedian*
1741 David Garrick, *The Lying Valet*   **1747** *Miss in Her Teens*   **1753 Samuel Foote,***The Englishman in Paris*
*Englishman returned from Paris***1756**
1757 *The Author*

1749 Henry Fielding, *The History of Tom Jones*
1751 *Amelia, Increase of Robbers*
1752 *Convent Garden Journal*
1755 *Journal of a Voyage to Lisbon*
1751 Tobias George Smollett, *The Adventure of Peregrine Pickle*
1753 *Ferdinand Count Fanthom*

1740	1741	1742	1743	1744	1745	1746	1747	1748	1749	1750	1751	1752	1753	1754	1755	1756	1757	1758	1759

1760 George II ✞; George III-first Hanoverian monarch   1775 War of Independence
1761 William Pitt resigned and the peace party gained control of the government
1762 (-63) John Stuart, Earl of Bute, became prime minister (Tories)
1763 John Wilke began his career as champion of popular liberties
1765 **Stamp Act,** a tax imposed on all legal documents to finance a
stricter colonial administration and the debts of the late colonial war

1760 **Population** estim. 8 million   **1750 to 1790**   1600 Acts of Parliament to improve the 24.000 miles of turnpike roads

1766 **Anti-British riots** in the colonies forced the government
to repeal the Stamp Act
1762 *Bridgewater Canal*   1767 **American Import Duties Act:** tax imposed by parliament on glass, tea, etc.
(efforts to increase the rate of transported goods)   in the colonies
1768 (-70) ●First voyage of James Cook to Australia / New Zealand
●Royal Academy was founded with Sir Joshua Reynolds as president
1770 (-82) ●Lord North's ministry was backed by
George III and his `friends´;
1769 J. Watt patents his **first steam engine**
●American duties were repealed except for tea

E C O N O M I C S   1767 James Stuart. Principles of Political Economy
1767   1769   cotton industry: process of mechanisation   1779
Hargreave's Spinning Jenny   Arkwright's Water Frame   Crompton's Mule
Adam Smith An inquiry of nature and causes of the wealth of nations   1776
Thomas Malthus ✳ 1766   David Ricardo ✳ 1772

1773 ●*Boston Tea Party* was a protest
against the tea tax;
●John Howard began his prison reforms
1774 Edmund Burke made his
orations on American taxation
**1776 Declaration of
Independence**
France joined America in **war against England 1778**
Spain   declared war against England   1779

The Industrial Revolution was born in the Severn River Valley. In its glory days, this valley — blessed with abundant deposits of iron ore and coal, and a river for transport — gave the world its first iron wheels, steam-powered locomotive, and cast-iron bridge. The museums in **Ironbridge Gorge**, which capture the flavor of the Victorian Age, take you back into the days when Britain was racing into the modern era — and pulling the rest of the West with her.

Romanticism

1764 ✳ Ann Radcliffe   1771 ✳ Sir Walter Scott   1775 ✳ Jane Austen
1760 ✳ William Beckford   Thomas Chatterton ✞ 1770 1771   1775 ✳ Charles Lamb
Edward Young ✞ 1765   Oliver Goldsmith ✞ 1774   1778
William Shenstone ✞ **1763**   Laurence Sterne ✞ **1768**   David Hume ✞ **1776**   ✳ William Hazlitt
1770 ✳ William Wordsworth   David Garrick ✞ 1797
1774 ✳ Robert Southey   Campbell
1772 ✳ S.T.Coleridge   1777 ✳ Thomas
✳ Thomas Moore 1779

1771 *Encyclopaedia Britannica*
William Cowper, *Olney Hyms* **1779**
Thomas Percy, *Reliques of Ancient English Poetry*
1765 James Macpherson, *Ossian*
1768 Thomas Gray, *Poems*
1768 Sterne *A Sentimental Journey through France and Italy by*
1770 Goldsmith *The Deserted Village*
1771 Tobias G. Smollett, *The Expedition of Humphrey Clinker*
1765 Walpole, *The Castle of Otranto*   Henry Mackenzie, *Man of Feeling* **1778**
Editor of *The Plays of William Shakespeare*   Frances Burney **1778**
1766 Goldsmith *The Vicar of Wakefield*   *Evelina, or a Young lady´s Entrance*
1760(-´67) Sterne *The Life and Opinions of Tristram Shandy, (-69) Gentleman Mr. Yorick*   *into the World*
1773 Goldsmith *The Stoops to Conquer
or the Mistake of a Night*
1775 Sheridan *The Rivals*
1767 Goldsmith *The Good Nature´d Man*   1777 Sheridan
1766 George Colman, *The Clandestine Marriage*   *School for Scandal*

| 1780 | 1781 | 1782 | 1783 | 1784 | 1785 | 1786 | 1787 | 1788 | 1789 | 1790 | 1791 | 1792 | 1793 | 1794 | 1795 | 1796 | 1797 | 1798 | 1799 | 1800 |

1783 Tory Government William Pitt, the Younger (1759-1806)

1780 *Sea War* against Netherlands.

1783 The Treaties of Paris and Versailles
ended the **War of American Independence**.

1783-1801 **William Pitt the Younger** (1759-1806)
and the New Tories formed Pitt`s First Ministry.

1784 The *Treaty of Paris* ended the.
Fourth Sea War against Netherlands.

1785 Pitt´s proposals for parliamentary
reform were rejected by his party.
Pitt effected financial reforms.

1787 The **Society for the Abolition
of the Slave Trade** was founded

1788 First **penal colony in
Botany Bay** (Sidney).

1789 The *French Revolution* began.

1792 **France declared war** against Austria
and Prussia.

1793 **France declared war** against England.
War with France in the West Indies

Louis XVI was executed.
Muir and Palmer were
transported to Botany
Bay for advocating reforms.

1795 **Seditious Meetings
Acts,** restricted
open political discussion

Napoleon conquered Italy and the English evacuated the Mediterranean **1796**

Nelson defeated Napoleon´s fleet at the mouth of the Nile, and reoccupied Mediterranean waters **1798**

Reform societies were suppressed by acts of parliament. **1799**

Adam Smith ✝ 1790

1785 cotton industry: process of mechanisation 1793
Cartwright's Power Loom   Whitney's Cotton Gin

1785 The publisher **John Walter** founded **The Daily Universal Register**, renamed as **Times 1788**

1780 **Robert Raikes** opened the *first Sunday schools*

Thomas Pains 1792 1793 **William Godwin,** *Enquiry concerning*
Age of Reason   *Political Justice*
A Journey through Holland **1795**

Industrial Revolution named by **A. Toynbee**: technical inventions increased condition of transport systems; change from cottage production to factory production; change of social classes; more and better usage of arable land. Working at night in factories is possible with gas lightning; change of working habits due to shift work

1786 Th. R. Malthus, *Theoretical Thoughts about Population Growth*
An Essay on the Principles of Population **1798**

1789 J. Bentham, *Introduction to the Principles of Morals and*
Legislation

1790 Edmund Burke, *Reflections on the French Revolution*

1791 Thomas Paine, *Rights of Man*

1792 Mary Shelley, *A Vindication of the Rights*
of Women –

John Constable, 1776-1837 often considered as the first impressionist (Hampstead Heath, Rainbow, Coast near Brighton)
William Turner, 1775-1851, was the most original landscape painter (Gypsy Camp, Garden of Hesperides)

Gothic Novel

S. Johnson ✝ **1784**

1784 ❋ Leigh Hunt

1788 ❋ Lord Byron

J. Wesley ✝ **1791**

1792 ❋ Percy Bysshe Shelley

1795 ❋ John Keats

Robert Burns ✝ **1796**
James Macpherson ✝ **1796**

Romanticism

1793 ❋ John Clare   H. Walpole ✝ 1797

1786 Robert Burns, *Poems Chiefly in the Scottish Dialect*

1783 George Crabbe, *The Village*

1772- **1882 William Mason** (?), *The English Garden*

1789 William Blake,
Songs of Innocence

1794 *Songs of Experience*
1793 Robert Southey, *Joan of Arc*

William Wordsworth and S. T. Coleridge, *Lyrical Ballads* **1798**

1785 William Cowper, *The Task*

The Prelude **1798**

Thomas Campbell (1777-1844) together with **Wordsworth**, *Lyrical Ballads* **1798**

1794 Mrs. Hannah Cowley (1743-1809)
The Town before You

1794 Robert Southey, *The Fall of Robbespierre*

1794 Richard Cumberland, *The Jews*

1795 *The Wheel of Fortune*

Gregory Lewis, *The Castle Spectre* **1797**

1786 William Beckford Matthew
The History of Caliph Vathek **Joanna Baillie**, *Plays on the Passions* **1798**

1791 John O`Keefe, *Wild Oats*

1794 Anne Radcliffe, *The Mysteries*
of Udolpho

1791 William Gilpin, *Remarks on*
Forest Scenery, and other Woodland Views

Matthew Gregory Lewis (Monk Lewis), *Ambrosio??, or the Monk* **1796**

John Colman (the Younger) (1762-1836), *The Heir at Law* **1797**

| 1780 | 1781 | 1782 | 1783 | 1784 | 1785 | 1786 | 1787 | 1788 | 1789 | 1790 | 1791 | 1792 | 1793 | 1794 | 1795 | 1796 | 1797 | 1798 | 1799 | 1780 |

1800 1801 1802 1803 1804 1805 1806 1807 1808 1809 1810 1811 1812 1813 1814 1815 1816 1817 1818 1819 1820

1800 Pitt´s **Combination Acts** rendered trade unionism illegal

1800~**Symbolism**

1804 Horticultural Society founded in London

1800 nearly 3.000 miles of canals completed- national income £ 230 m ⇒ **1830** £ 350 m

1806 ✳ **John Stuart Mill**   ✳ **Karl Marx**   **1818**
1810 David Ricardo *The High Price of Bullion…*
                                        1817 *Principles of Politi
cal Economy and Taxation*

Romanticism

Windsor Castle
The largest castle in England. Standing on a hill of chalk near the Thames, it was originally built to guard London's approaches. The castle has grown continuously since it was established by William the Conqueror. Edward III considerably enlarged the Royal apartments in Upper Ward, and founded St George's Chapel. An immense amount of restoration and embellishment was undertaken under George III, George IV and Victoria, and much of what is seen today is the creation of this period - the great Round Tower as built by Henry II was much lower and many towers in Upper Ward were built or heightened during the Gothic restorations by Sir Jeffry Wyatville in the early 19th century.

1800 1801 1802 1803 1804 1805 1806 1807 1808 1809 1810 1811 1812 1813 1814 1815 1816 1817 1818 1819 1820

1800 ✝ William Cowper   Thomas Percy ✝1811 **1812**✳ Robert Browning   **1819**
Richard Cumberland ✝ 1811 **1812**✳ Charles Dickens   ✳ George Eliot
1803 ✳ Edward G.E. Bulwer-Lytton   Richard Brinsley Sheridan ✝ **1816**
1809 ✳ Alfred Lord Tennyson **1814**✳ Charles Reade
1806 ✳ Elizabeth Barrett-Browning   **1815** ✳ Anthony Trollope
1809 ✳Edward Fitzgerald   **1816** Charlotte Brontë
1804 ✳ Benjamin Disraeli   **1811** ✳ William Makepeace Thackeray   **1818**✳
1810 ✳ Elizabeth C. Gaskell   Emily Jane Brontë
Matthew G. Lewis ✝ **1818** **1819**

✳ Charles Kingsley

1801 Lewis *Tales of Wonder*   **1808 Lamb** *Adventures of Ulysses*   **1817 Hazlitt** *The*
1808 *Specimens of English Dramatic*   *Characters of Shakespeare's Plays*
Poets who lived about the   **1819**
Time of Shakespeare   **Keats** *Otho the Great; King Stephen*
1805 Godwin *Fleetwood*   **1810 Scott** *The Lady of the Lake*   **1817 Byron** *Manfred*
1801 Moore *The Poetical Works of the late Thomas Little Esq.*   **1817 Keats** *Poems*
1806 Moore *Epistles, Odes, and other Poems*   **1816 Peacock** *Headlong Hall*
1817 *Melincourt*
1817 Godwin
Mandeville
1814 Scott *Waverley*   **1818 Scott**
1811 Austen *Sense and Sensibility*   *Rob Roy*
1813 *Pride and*   *The Heart of Midlothian*
Prejudice   **1818 Austen**
Mansfield Park **1814;**   *Northanger Abbey*
1818
Wollstonecraft-Shelley *Frankenstein*
1813 Coleridge *Remorse*

1820 1821 1822 1823 1824 1825 1826 1827 1828 1829 1830 1831 1832 1833 1834 1835 1836 1837 1838 1839 1840

1821 Monroe-Doctrine   **1827** Canning Prime Minister   **1832** First Parliamentary Reform Act
1828 Wellington Prime Minister

1833 First Factory Law limits children labour to 9
hours a day, 48 hours a week
1833 beginning of the Oxford Movement
1833 abolition of slavery in the colonies
1834 Poor Law Amendment Act
beginning of the Chartists' Movement in the **1836**
"London Working Men's Association"

William IV ✝ **1837**
Passing of the "Anti-Corn-Law-League" **1838**
●Parliament refused to accept the demands of the Chartists **1839**
!First British Steamship to New York!**1838**
●Public disturbances were supressed

Romanticism / Realism

W. Turner "The Temeraire"**1838**

1822 1823 J. Constable "The Leaping Horse"

1833 Ch. Lyell, *Principles of Geology*

David Ricardo✝ 1823

Jeremy Bentham ✝ **1832** Utilitarianism: 'Society should be governed
by the principle of the greatest happiness for the greatest number.'

1820✳ Herbert Spencer   **1825** ✳ Thomas Henry Huxley   **1834** ✳ William Morris
1821 ✝ John Keats   **1828** ✳ George Meredith   **1837** ✳ Algernon
1822 ✳ Matthew Arnold   Samuel Taylor Coleridge ✝ **1834**   Charles Swinburne
1822 ✳ Percy Bysshe Shelley ✝ William Hazlitt ✝ **1830**   Walter Pater ✳ **1839**
George Gordon Byron ✝ **1824**   Sir Walter Scott ✝ **1832**   **1835** ✳ Samuel Butler
1820 ✳ Anne Brontë   William Blake ✝ **1827** **1828** ✳ Dante Gabariel Rossetti   **1834** ✳ James Thomson
Charles Robert Maturin✝ **1824**   **1830** ✳ Christina Georgina Rossetti
1820 ✳ Anne Brontë   **1829** ✳ Thomas William Robertson
1820 Keats *La belle Dame sans Merci*   **1827** Tennyson *Poems, by Two Brothers*
1820 Keats *Lamia and other Poems*   **1830** Tennyson *Poems, chiefly lyrical*
1820 P.B. Shelley *Prometheus Unbound*   **1832** Tennyson *Poems (The Lotus Eaters*
1821 G. G. Byron *Cain*   **1833** R. Browning *Pauline*
1821 G. G. Byron *Heaven and Earth*)
1821 Wordsworth *Ecclesiastical Sonnets*
1822 G. G. Byron *The Vision of Judgement*
1822 W. Blake *The Whirlwind*

1820 Walter Scott *Ivanhoe*   **1825** Carlyle *The Life of Schiller* **1830** Carlyle *On History*   **1836** Th. Carlyle *Sartor*
1821 Shelley *A Defence of Poetry*   **1827** Carlyle *German Romance*   **1833** Carlyle *On History Again*   *Resartus*
1821 Walter Scott *Kenilworth*   **1828** Carlyle *Essay on Burns*   **1837** Carlyle *The*
1821 Th. de Quincey *Confessions of an English Opium-Eater*   **1833** Disraeli *Alroy*   *French Revolution*
1826 Disraeli *Vivian Grey*   **1831** Disraeli *The Young Duke*   **1838** Carlyle
1828 Dickens *Oliver Twist*   *Lectures on the History of Literature*
1832 Disraeli *Contarini Fleming*   *Essay on Scott*
1839
Carlyle *Lectures on European Revolutions*
1833 *J.St. Mill Thoughts on Poetry and its* **1839**
Varieties   Carlyle *Chartism*
1837 Disraeli
Henrietta Temple
1837 *Venetia*
1835 Dickens *Sketches by Boz*
1837 Dickens *The*
Posthumous Papers of the PickwickClub
1836 W.M. Thackeray
Yellowplush Papers
Dickens *Nicholas Nickelby* **1838**

1820 C.R. Maturin *Melmouth the Wanderer*   **1829** D. Jerrold *Black-Eyed Susan*

1820 1821 1822 1823 1824 1825 1826 1827 1828 1829 1830 1831 1832 1833 1834 1835 1836 1837 1838 1839 1840

1840 1841 1842 1843 1844 1845 1846 1847 1848 1849 1850 1851 1852 1853 1854 1855 1856 1857 1858 1859 1860

1840 Queen Victoria marries Prince Albert of Saxe-Coburg Gotha   **1851** The Great Exhibition in London

      1842 Mines Act bans women and children   **1854** Cholera epidemic kills 52.293

        under 10 from working under ground   people

           1844 Factory Act limits female workers to 12-hour day,   **1857** Matrimonial

            8-13 olds to 6½ hours   Causes Act:

            Ragged schools for poor children introduced   divorce courts

                1846 Potato failure leads to severe famine in Ireland set up in England

                1847 Factory Act limits children aged 13-18   & Wales

                  and women to 10-hour day

                  Chloroform used as an anaesthetic for the first time

                1848 Public Health Act improves sanitation

Population   **1851** **21** million

                                              1859

                                 J. St. Mill. On Liberty

      1842 ✳ Alred Marshall

CULTURE

         1844 W. Turner "Rain, *Steam And Speed*" (Painting)

           1846 Daily News founded with Charles Dickens as editor

               1849 Bedford College for Women, London, established

                           1855 Daily Telegraph published

                               for the first time

                            1858

                 Charles Darwin and Alfred Russel

         announce theory of evolution of species

               W. Morris *Queen Guinevera* (Paint.)

            D.G. Rossetti *Queen Guinevera* (Paint)

Palace of Westminster with the Victoria Tower (left) and the Elizabeth Tower (right)

The Houses of Parliament

      Emily Bronte   ✝ **1848**   **1850** ✳ Robert Louis Stevenson   **1856** ✳ Oscar Wilde

        Anne Bronte ✝**1849**   Charlotte Bronte ✝ **1855**

       Mary Wollstonecraft-Shelley   ✝ **1851**

   1843 ✳ Henry James   Thomas Moore   ✝ **1852**

1840 ✳ Thomas Hardy   William Wordsworth   ✝**1850**

    1843 William Wordsworth *Poet Laureate*   **1850** A. Tennyson *Poet Laureate*

             1850 A. Tennyson *In Memoriam*   *Life of Charlotte Brontë*

     1844 Thackeray *The Luck of Barry Lyndon*   **1857** Gaskell *The*

           1852 Thackeray *The History of Henry Esmond*

              1853 E. Gaskell *Ruth*   **1857** *The Virginians*

1841 Dickens *Master Humphrey's Clock*   **1848** Thackeray *The Book of Snobs*   **1859**

      1847 Charlotte Brontë *Jane Eyre*   George Eliot *Adam Bede*

               A. Tennyson *Idylls Of The King* **1859** - 1885

   1842 Dickens *American Notes*   **1853** Dickens *Bleak House*   **1854** Dickens *Hard Times*

1840 Thackeray *The Paris Sketch Book*   **1847** Emily Brontë *Wuthering Heights*   **1857** *Little Dorrit*

  1843 Dickens *A Christmas Carol* **1848** W.M. Thackeray *Vanity Fair*   **1859**

1841 Thackeray *History of Samuel Titmarsh* **1848** E. Gaskell *Mary Barton*   Dickens *A Tale of Two Cities*

   1844 Dickens *Martin Chuzzlewit* **1849** Charlotte Bronte *Shirley*   **1855** Gaskell *North and South*

     1845 Dickens *The Chimes*   **1850** Dickens *David Copperfield*

1841 Dickens *The Old Curiosity Shop* **1847** Dickens *Dombey and Son* **1852** W.M. Thackeray *Henry Esmond*   **1859**

    1845 Disraeli *Sybil, or The Two Nations*   **1853** Gaskell *Ruth*   Gaskell *Lois, the Witch*

        1848 Gaskell *Mary Barton*   **1853** Gaskell *Cranford*

1840 1841 1842 1843 1844 1845 1846 1847 1848 1849 1850 1851 1852 1853 1854 1855 1856 1857 1858 1859

1860 1861 1862 1863 1864 1865 1866 1867 1868 1869 1870 1871 1872 1873 1874 1875 1876 1877 1878 1879 1880

1877 Queen
Victoria becomes Empress of India

Prime Ministers

| Palmerston | 1865 | 1868 | Gladstone | 1874 | Disraeli 1880 |

- Britain didn't dominate the international scene as they did in earlier periods
- England's international importance was overshadowed by modern Italy, the American Civil War and Germany under Bismarck
- political mood was based on forceful opportunism
- a demand for a new and active liberalism was gaining ground
- the death of Palmerston was followed by the reopening of the reform question and eventually by the passing of the second Reform bill in **1867**

1866 Gladstone introduced Reform Bill, which was severely mauled by the Conservatives and some anti-reform Liberals, who were led by Robert Lowe and later became the "Cave of Adullam"

1867 Second Reform bill Ireland

1870 disestablishment and partial disendowment of the Church of

1870 W.E. Forster's **Elementary Education Act** establishes dual Church and state control of schools

1871 University Test Act

Palmerston ✝ **1865**

1871 Civil Service, with the exception of the Foreign Office, is thrown open to competitive examination

1872 Ballot Act introducing secret ballot for all parliamentary and municipal elections

1873 Judicature Act (amended in 1876) simplifies the forest of legal institutions and procedures

1875 Public Health Act creates

1867 government resigns and Lord Derby and Disraeli a public health authority take over for the third of their minority governments in every area

1875 Employers and Workmen Act, masters and men are placed on equal footing as regards breaches of

1868 majority votes for Gladstone contract **1878**

1865 - 1868 John Stuart Mill M.P. for Westminster Factory act

1869 Thomas Arnold *Culture & Anarchy* **1876** Leslie Stephen *History Of English Thought In The 18th Century*

E C O N O M I C S Doctrine of Marginal Utility W.S. Jevons Theory of Political Economy; Carl Menger Grundsätze der Volkswirtschaftslehre; Leon Walras Elements d'Economie PolitiquePure

1867 Karl Marx Capital, I

1861 ✝Elizabeth Browning **1865** ✳ Rudyard Kipling

1865 ✳ William Butler Yeats

1863 William Makepeace Thackeray ✝

Charles Dickens ✝ **1870**

Thomas William Robertson ✝ **1871**

1872 ✳ Aubrey Vincent Beardsley

1874 ✳ Gilbert Keith Chesterton

1873 ✳ Walter John de la Mare

1878 ✳
John Masefield

1871/72 George Eliot *Middlemarch* James *Daisy Miller*

1872 Thomas Hardy *Under the Greenwood Tree***1879**

1872 Butler *The Way of all Flesh* Meredith *The Egoist*

1872 Carroll *Through the Looking Glass* **1879**

1874 Thomas Hardy *Far From The*

1871 Charles Dickens *The Mystery Madding Crowd*

1874-76 Eliot *Daniel Deronda*

1866 Gaskell *Wives and Daughters* of Edwin Drood **1878**

1864/65 Charles Dickens *Our Mutual Friend* Thomas Hardy *The Return Of The Native*

1861 George Eliot *Silas Marner***1866** George Eliot *Felix Holt* **1875** James *A Passionate Pilgrim*

1863 George Eliot *Romola* **1869** Carroll *Phantasmagoria* **1876** H. James *Roderick*

1860 George Eliot *The Mill On The Floss* **1877** Hudson

1860/61 Charles Dickens *Great Expectations* James *The American*

1863 Gaskell *Sylvia's Lover* **1872** Butler *Erewhon* **1878** James *The Europeans*

1864 Robertson *David Garrick* **1869** Robertson *School*

1865 Robertson *Society* **1869** Robertson *Home*

1866 Robertson *Ours* **1870** Robertson *M.P.*

1867 Robertson *Caste*

1868 Robertson *Play*

1860 1861 1862 1863 1864 1865 1866 1867 1868 1869 1870 1871 1872 1873 1874 1875 1876 1877 1878 1879 1880

| 1880- | Gladstone | 1885/1886 | | Salisbury | 1892 | | 1895 | Salisbury |

- England dreamt of territorial expansion
- Between 1884 and 1902 2,500,000 sq. miles of territory fell under British control

1881 Transvaal rebellion (Engl. colony)

1881 Gladstone declares independence of the Boers under a vague British sovereignty

1886 Whigs and Radicals allied themselves against Gladstone
because of the impact of the Irish question on English politics
and the problems of imperial policy (-> the Transvaal question)

1886 Salisbury: conservative prime minister (1886-1892 and 1895-1902)

1887 Victoria's jubilee: demonstration of national patriotism and imperial pride

1895 Jameson Raid:
Englishmen crossed into
Transvaal territory again
because of the opening of
the Transvaal gold fields

Victorias second jubilee: **1897**
differences of
opinion between
the colonies
concerning politics,
trade and defence

1899
war between England and Boer in South Africa

1883 John Maynard Keynes

A. Marshall 1897

1890 The Principle of Economics   **The Pure Theory of Foreign Trade**

Karl Marx ✝1883 Class War: 'Society is made up of classes in perpetual struggle.'

Naturalism

Antony
Trollope ✝ **1882**

Robert Louis Stevenson ✝ **1894**

1884 ✳ Sean O'Casey **1888** ✳ Thomas Stearns Eliot   **1894** ✳ John Priestley   **1899**

1880 George Eliot ✝   **1885** ✳ D.H. Lawrence   **1891** ✳Agatha Christie   ✳ Noël Coward

1882 ✳ Virginia Woolf   **1888** ✳ Katherine Mansfield   **1894** ✳ John Priestley

1882 ✳ James Joyce   **1888** ✳ Joyce Cary   **1892** ✳ Victoria Sackville-West

1880 ✳ G. Strachey   **1886** ✳ Siegfried Sassoon   **1892** ✳ Ivy Compton-Burnett

1883 ✳ Th. Hulme   Walter Pater✝ **1894** ✳ Aldous Huxley

Thomas   Edward Lear ✝ **1888**   **1893** ✳Wilfred Owen;

Carlyle ✝**1881**   Matthew Arnold ✝ **1888**   **1892**✳ Richard Aldington

Lewis Carroll ✝ **1898**

1881 Oscar Wilde *Poems*   *Ballad of Reading Gaol***1898**

1881 H. James *The Portrait of a Lady*   **1888** Thomas Hardy *Wessex Tales*   *What Maisie Knew*

1880 Hardy *The Trumpet-Major*   **1886** Thomas Hardy *The Mayor of Casterbridge*   **1897** H. James

1882 Hardy *Two on a Tower*   **1891** Thomas Hardy *Life's Little Ironies*   **1898** James

1887 Thomas Hardy *The Woodlanders*   *The Turn of the Screw*

1883 Stevenson *Treasure Island*   **1896** Thomas Hardy *Jude*

1886 Stevenson *The Strange Case of Dr. Jekyll and Mr Hyde*   *the Obscure*

1886 Stevenson *Kidnapped*   **1891** Thomas Hardy *Tess of the d'Urbervilles*

1891 Oscar Wilde *The Picture Of Dorian Gray*

1889 Stevenson *The Master of Ballantrae*   **1897** Conrad *The*

1893 Stevenson *Catriona*   *Nigger of the*

1893 *Island Night Entertainment*   *Narcissus*

1892 Oscar Wilde *Lady Windermere's Fan*

1893 *A Woman of No Importance*

1895 *The Importance of being*

1893 *Salomé*   *Earnest*

1914 World War I 1918

Prime Ministers: Salisbury Balfour Campell-Bannermann Asquith George; Conservative | Liberal | Coalition

1904 Entente Cordiale (Britain & France) **1912** New Home Rule Bill   **1918**

1900 Foundation of Labour Party   **1911** Parliament Act   Representation of the

1902 End of South African War   National Insurance Act (George)   People Act

1919

Extent of the British Empire before World War I: Peace treaty of Versailles

Surface: 31,6 Mio. qkm (= 24% of the earth surface)   **1914** Entente of France, Russia &

Population: 502 Mio people (=25% of mankind)   Britain faces Alliance of Germany;

Austria-Hungary & Italy;

Foreign policy: growth of self-government in the colonies and dominions   invasion of Belgium by Germany:

Herbert Spencer ✝ 1903   Social Darwinism: 'Society is made up of social organisms subject to the survival of the fittest.'

British strike statistics: annual averages   Union membership

Number

Number ofWorkers involved   Strike-days   (000s)

strikes   (000)   (000)   1892   1.576

1900-   10   529   240   4.576   1900   2.022

1911-   13   1.074   1.034   20.908   1910   2.565

1914-   18   844   632   5.292   1913   4.135

1919   21   1.241   2.108   49.053   1917   5.499

1920   8.348

George Gissing✝ **1903** Algernon Charles Swinburne✝ **1909**   Henry James ✝ **1916**   **1919**

Oscar Wilde ✝ **1900**   George Meredith✝ **1909**   **1914** ✻ Dylan Thomas   ✻ Iris Murdoch

John Ruskin ✝ **1900**   **1906** ✻ Samuel Beckett   **1911** ✻ William Golding   **1919**

1903 ✻ George Orwell   **1907** ✻ Christopher Fry   **1912** ✻ Lawrence Durrell   ✻ Doris Lessing

Samuel Butler ✝ **1902**   **1904** ✻ Graham Greene   **1909** ✻ Stephen Spender

1903 ✻ Evelyn Waugh   **1907**✻ Wystan Hugh Auden   Rupert Brooke ✝ **1915**

1904 ✻ Christopher Isherwood   **1913** ✻ Angus Wilson

1907 ✻ Daphne du Maurier

1905 ✻ C.P.Snow

1907 ✻ Louis MacNeice

1904 William Butler Yeats *In the Seven Woods*   **1914 Th. Hardy** *Satires of Circumstance*

1914 W. B. Yeats *Responsibilities*

1902 Gibson *Mountain Lovers*   **1910 Yeats** *The Green Helmet and Other Poems*

1909 *Hardy:Time's Laughing-Stocks and other Verses*

1917 T.S. Eliot,

Prufrock

1901 Thomas Hardy *Poems of the Past and Present*

1910 Masefield *Poems a. Ballads* **1915 Aldington** *Images, Old and*

1913 Hulme *Complete Poetical Works*   *New*

1911 Sassoon *Twelve Sonnets*

1900 Joseph Conrad, *Lord Jim*   **1907** *The Secret Agent*   **1914 James Joyce,** *Dubliners*

1901 Kipling *Kim* **1904 Joseph Conrad** *Nostromo*   **1918** *Exiles*

1901 Herbert George Wells, *The First Men in the Moon*   **1913 David Herbert Lawrence,** *Sons and*

1905 *A Modern Utopia*   **1910 E. M. Forster** *Howards End*   *Lovers*

1902 James *The Wings of the Dove***1907 E. M. Forster,** *The Longest Journey*   **1915** *The Rainbow*

1901 Bennett *Anna of the Five Towns***1907 Bennett** *The Grim Smile of the Five Towns*   **1918**

1902 Bennett *The Grand Babylon Hotel***1908 Bennett** *The Old Wives' Tale*   **Mansfield** *Prelude*

1903 Bennett *The Truth about an Author*   **1911 Bennett** *The Card*

1905 Bennett *Tales of the Five Towns***1911 Bennett** *Hilda Lessways* **1916 Bennett** *These Twain*

1905 E.M.Forster *Where Angels fear to Tread*

1911 Katherine Mansfield *In a German Pension*

1901 Ford Madox Ford *The Inheritors*   **1908 Bennett** *Buried Alive* **Mansfield** *Je ne parle pas Francais*   **1918**

1903 Ford *Romance* (with **Conrad**)   **1910 Bennett** *Clayhanger*   **1915 V. Woolf** *The Voyage Out*

1903 James *The Ambassadors***1908 E. M. Forster** *A Room with a View*   **1919**

1904 James *The Golden Bowl*   **Virginia Woolf** *Night and Day*

1903 Thomas Hardy *The Dynasts*   **1911** *The White Peacock*

1905 E. M. Forster *Where Angels Fear to Tread*

1901 Wells *The First Men in the Moon*   **1910 Wells** *The History of Mr Polly*

1900 William Butler Yeats, *The Shadowy Waters*   **1909 Pinero** *Mid-Channell*

1901 George Bernard Shaw, *Three Plays for Puritans*   **1912** *Pygmalion*

1904 John Galsworthy *The Island Pharisees*   **Galsworthy** *Beyond* **1917**

1911 Galsworthy *The Patrician*

1907 Galsworthy *The Country House* **1913 Galsworthy** *The Dark Flower*

1920   George V   1936 Edward VIII 1936 George VI 1940

1920	1921	1922	1923	1924	1925	1926	1927	1928	1929	1930	1931	1932	1933	1934	1935	1936	1937	1938	1939	1940

1920-22 Coalition Conservatives and Liberals under Lloyd George (Liberal).   **1935-37** National Government
     1922-23 Conservatives under Bonar Law   **1929-31**: Labour under MacDonald   under Baldwin
        1923: Stanley Baldwin succeeds Law. short Labour government (ten month Governments and prime ministers)
           1924-29: Conservatives under Baldwin   **1931-35**:National Government under MacDonald
                                                     1937-39
                     National Government under Neville Chamberlain

Monarchs: King George V(1920-36)   King Edward VIII(1936) King George VI(1936-40)

1920: Government of Ireland Act (Irish Home Rule)   **1929**: General election: Labour gains plurality; Worldwide economic crisis
met with resistance by the IRA;   (New York 'Black Friday') also affects Britain, the years of depression begin.
1920 Climax of membership in trade unions: 8million.
     1921:Climax of unemployment: 2 million;   **1928**: India wants to maintain the status of dominion
Black Friday: wages standstill   **1934**: Unemployment Act
King George formally opens the new Northern   (reorganisation of relief system).
Ireland parliament.   **1927**: General strikes are prohibited by law.
       1922: Egypt and Ireland become independent; BBC founded.   **1932**: Problems with elections in India
         1923: General election: Labour wins and forms   Mahatma Gandhi wants to fast to death
     first Labour government in British history;   J.Galsworthy receives Nobel Prize for literature
        1923 W.B. Yeats receives Nobel Prize for literature.
           1924: General election: The Conservatives return.   **1935**: General election
            1925: G.B.Shaw receives Nobel Prize for literature.   National government confirmed.
             1926: Coal mining and transport unions start general strike due to a 'freeze' of wages, but after
Baldwin offered a compromise the strike ends; the dominions become self-governing
communities in 'The British Commonwealth of Nations'.
                     1930: The Statute of Westminster (British monarch is head of all
Commonwealth nations); priority customs for the dominions.
                  1931: 23% of insured workers unemployed; MacDonald
resigns but is persuaded to form the National Government.
                      1933: End of depression(drop in production
                         from 1929 to 1932 was 16%);
                          unemployment is reduced.

                King George V✝ **1936** Begin of British
                        Appeasement Policy.
                    1937: E.M. Forster
                 receives Benson Medal for literature.
                     1938
Munich Conference (Chamberlain seeks negotiations with Hitler and Mussolini); peak of
appeasement policy; as Germany invades Czechoslovakia British policy is reversed.
                         1939
England enters second World War on September 3rd.

                   1930 J.M. Keynes. *Treatise on Money* **1936** *The General Theory*

    J. Conrad   ✝   **1924**   D.H.Lawrence   ✝**1930**   W.B.Yeats   ✝   **1939**
K.Mansfield   ✝**1923**   T.Hardy   ✝ **1928**   J.Galsworthy   ✝   **1933**
                                         1930 ✳ Harold Pinter
                     1928 ✳ A.Sillitoe   **1933** ✳ Penelope Lively

Poetry:
     1921 W.B.Yeats, *Michael Robartes and the dancer*   .**1930** T.S. Eliot, *Ash Wednesday*
       1922 T.S.Eliot, *The Waste Land.*   **1934** Dylan Thomas, *Eighteen Poems*
           1925 Thomas Hardy, *Collected Poems.*   1936 W.H. Auden,   *Look*
             1928 W.B.Yeats,*The Tower.*   *Stranger*

1920 D.H.Lawrence, *Women in Love.*   **1931** Virginia Woolf, *The Waves*
     1922 James Joyce, *Ulysses.. ..*   J.R.R. Tolkien **1938** ,
     1922 Katherine Mansfield, *The Garden Party*   *The Hobbit*
        1924 E.M. Forster, *A passage to India.*   **1932** Aldous Huxley, *Brave New World*
     1922 Virginia Woolf, *Jacobs Room*   **1928** D.H.Lawrence, *Lady Chatterley's Love*
     1922 John Galsworthy, *The Forsyte Saga*   **1934** Graham Greene, *Its a Battlefield.*
                                      1937 George
                         Orwell, *The Road to Wigans Pier.*
                                1938
                         Samuel Beckett, *Murphy*
                                   1939
                        James Joyce, *Finnegans Wake*
        1924 George Bernard Shaw, *Saint Joan.*   **1935** T.S.Eliot, *Murder in the*
                                             Cathedral

1920	1921	1922	1923	1924	1925	1926	1927	1928	1929	1930	1931	1932	1933	1934	1935	1936	1937	1938	1939	1940

1940 1941 1942 1943 1944 1945 1946 1947 1948 1949 1950 1951 1952 1953 1954 1955 1956 1957 1958 1959 1960

1939 World War II 1945

| **1940** | Conservatives | **1945** | Labour-Party | **1951** | | Conservatives | | |
| **1940** | Churchill | **1945** | Attlee | **1951** | Churchill | | **1955** Eden | **1957** Macmillan |

1940 British evacuation from Dunkirk **1946** National Health Service Act **1952** Reprivatisation of steel industry and road
1940 Italy declares war on Britain **1946** National Insurance Act transport
1940 Battle of Britain **1946** Nationalisation of Bank of England **1953** F.Crick and J.D.Watson identify
   1941 Anglo-Soviet agreement **1947** BBC starts regular TV programmes DNA as a carrier
   1941 Anglo-American Atlantic Charta **1947** Nationalization of power supply of genetic information
   1941 Britain and USA declare war on Japan **1948** Nationalization of gas supply **1954** End of rationing
      1942 British offensive in Africa **1949** Reform of franchise
      1942 Allies land in French North Africa **1949** Nationalisation of iron- and steel industry
         1943 Allies succeed in Africa **1951** Introduction of exams at end of school (GCE)
         1943 Allies land in Sicily **1952** First successful test of a British nuclear bomb
         1943 Armistice between Allies and Italy **1952** De-Havilland-aeroplane breaks sound barrier
            1944 Landing of Allies in Normandy **1954** Foundation of SEATO-Pact
               1945 Armistice between Allies and Japan **1955** Licence for commercial
               1945 Capitulation of Germany television ITV
                  1947 Nationalization of rail- and road transport **1956** Retreat of British
troops from zone
of Suez canal
1956 Franco-British
attack on Egypt stopped by UN
1957 Great
Britain refuses to join the EEC
1957 Five-day-
week in public service
1958 Life
Peerages Act
1958
Campaign for nuclear disarmament
1959
Permission for „Lady Chatterley's Lover"
(by D:H: Lawrence) to be published
1948 T.S. Eliot receives Nobel prize for Literature
1954 Composition of B.Britten's „The
Turn of the Screw"

John Maynard Keynes ✝ 1946   E C O N O M I C S

1941 James Joyce ✝   George Bernard Shaw ✝ **1950**
1941 Virginia Woolf ✝   George Orwell ✝ **1950**

            1949 G.Orwell; *1984*   **1954** K.Amis; *Lucky Jim*
            1949 A.Wilson; *The Wrong Set* **1954** W.Golding; *Lord of the Flies*
     1945 G.Orwell; *Animal Farm* **1955** S.Beckett; *Malone Dies*
1955 W.Golding; *Pincher Martin*
        1948 G.Greene; *The Heart of the Matter* **1955** I.Murdoch; *The Flight*
from the Enchanter

          1950 A.Wilson; *Such Darling Dodos* **1956** J.Braine; *Room at*
          1950 D.Lessing; *The Grass is Singing* *the Top*
1957 A.Sillitoe;
Saturday Night and Sunday Morning
            1953 J.Wain; *Hurry on Down* **1958**
The Loneliness of the Long-Distance Runner

1955 J.Osborne; *Look back in Anger*
1956 *The Entertainer*
1956 A.Wilson; *A Bit off*
the Map
1957 S.Beckett;
Endgame
1957 H.Pinter;
The Birthday Party
1957 A.Wesker;
The Wesker Trilogy (**1958-60**)
1958
J.Arden;Sergeant Musgrave's Dance

1940 1941 1942 1943 1944 1945 1946 1947 1948 1949 1950 1951 1952 1953 1954 1955 1956 1957 1958 1959 1960

1960 1961 1962 1963 1964 1965 1966 1967 1968 1969 1970 1971 1972 1973 1974 1975 1976 1977 1978 1979 1980

1961-63 Macmillan , Conservative   **1970-76** Edward Heath, Conservative
1963-66 Cabinett of Sir Alexander Douglas Home   **1976-76** Government coalition
1966-70 Wilson, Labour Party   Conservatives/Labour/Regionalists
                                       1976 Resignation of Wilson; successor
                                              J. Callaghan   **1979**
Government Callaghan brought down by motion of no confidence by the Conservatives under M. Thatcher
                                                                      1979
                              Election victory of the Conservatives under Margaret Thatcher

1960 Foundation of EFTA   **1965** Abolition of the capital punishment   **1972** Admittance to EEC   **1977** Silver
1960 Abolition of universal compulsory Military Service   **1971** "Immigration Bill"   Jubilee Elizabeth II
            1965 Foundation of the employer's association CBI**1973** Miner's Strike
            1967 Nationalization of the iron and steel industry
            1968 Laying down of the Immigration Act
1963 The Great Train Robbery   and the Act against Racial discrimination
1963 University reform   **1969** Reduction of the voting age
1963 Beginning of the Beatles-Era
      1966 Invention of the Mini-skirt by Mary Quant
   1965 Establishment of comprehensive schools all over Great Britain
      1966 England wins the Football World Championship
            1968 "Theatres Act" by Lord Chamberlain
            1968 C. Day Lewis becomes 'Poet Laureate'
               1969 Nobel Prize for Samuel Beckett
                  1970 Breakthrough of the feminist movement in Great Britain
                  1971 Establishment of the decimal currency
                     1972 J. Betjeman becomes 'Poet Laureate'
                        1975 Start of the North Sea oil
                                    production
                                    1979
                                    First test-tube baby

Queen Elizabeth II

Post-structuralism | Almost all colleges admit both girls and boys
a school of thought that emerged partly from within French structuralism in the 1960s, reacting against structuralist pretensions to scientific objectivity and comprehensiveness. The term coversthe philosophical deconstruction practised by Jacques Derrida and his followers, along with thelater works of the critic Roland Barthes, the psychoanalytic theories of Jacques Lacan and JuliaKristeva, the historical critiques of Michel Foucault, and the cultural-political writings of Jean-François Lyotard and Gilles Deleuze. These thinkers emphasized the instability of meanings andof intellectual categories, and sought to undermine any theoretical system that claimed to haveuniversal validity. They set out to dissolve the fixed binary oppositions of structuralist thought. Instead they favoured a non-hierarchical plurality or 'free play' of meanings, stressing the indeterminacy of texts.

Aldous Huxley ✝ **1963**   E.M. Forster ✝**1970**
            T.S. Eliot ✝**1965**
   Somerset Maugham   ✝ **1965**

                                 J.R.R. Tolkien   ✝ **1973**

Graham Greene
                                 1973 *The Honorary Consul*

Iris Murdoch
                                 1973 *The Black Prince*
                                       1976 *The Sacred and Profane Love Machine*
                                             1978 *The Sea*

Antony Burgess
      1962 *A Clockwork Orange*   **1967** *The Novel Now*
                                 1971 **E.M. Forster**. *Maurice*
Doris Lessing
      1962 *The Golden Notebook*

William Golding
            1966 *The Spire*

Edward Bond   **1965** *Saved*   **1968** *Early Morning*   **1973** *The Sea*   *The Woman*
         1962 **The Pope's Wedding**   **1971** *Lear*   **1976** *Bingo*   **1978** *The Bundle*
                              1968 *Narrow Road to the deep North*   **1975** *The Fool*
Harold Pinter
1960 *The Caretaker*   **1971** *Old Times*   **1975** *No Man s Land*
            1965 *The Homecoming*
                        1968 *Betrayal*
Samuel Beckett
      1961 *Happy Days*   **1967** *Come and Go*   **1972** *Not I*

1960 1961 1962 1963 1964 1965 1966 1967 1968 1969 1970 1971 1972 1973 1976 1975 1976 1977 1978 1979

1980 1981 1982 1983 1984 1985 1986 1987 1988 1989 1990 1991 1992 1993 1994 1995 1996 1997 1998 1999 2000

Prime Ministers

Conservatives Margaret Thatcher **1992** John Major 1997 Tony Blair

1980 race riots in Bristol
1980 heavy bomb attacks
   1981 Foundation of SDP
     1982 Falklands War
      1983 US-Missiles at Greenham Common

1987 no re-establishment of death penalty

        1989 Diplomatic relations with Argentina restored
      1988 Foundation of Social Liberal Democratic Party
           1997 Lady Di
            dies in car accident in Paris

     1986 longest Miner Strike **1990** "Poll-Tax"
(until March `**85**) Membership of EEC (until `**92**)
        1991 Error of justice: "Birmingham Six", "Maguire-Seven"
            NATO-Yougoslavia war **1999**

1986 race riots Outrage of IRA   **1992** Northern Irland-Conversation
   Border Gibraltar-Spain open   large peace-demonstration at Dublin
     1987 Participation in SDI   **1996** Inaguration of the Chan-
      1988 Building permit for the "Chunnel"   nel-Tunnel
        1993 Convention of Maastricht ratified

1981 Wedding Prince Charles and Lady Diana   **1990** G.Carey Archbishop of Canterbury
    1983 Nobel prize W.Golding   **1992** Separation of Charles and Diana
        50 year anniversary D Day **1996**

    1987 Ferry "Herald of Free Enterprise" capsizes at Zeebrugge **188** dead
Unemployment   **1988** Sabotaged airliner crashes on Lockerbie **270** dead
1980 2.000.000   **1991** Gulf War
1981 2.500.000   **1989** K.Ishiguro, The Remains of the Day (film)
1982 3.000.000   Beckett ✝ **1989**
1991 2.000.000   Golding✝ **1992**
1992 3.000.000   Greene ✝ **1991**
            Lively ✝ **1996**
          Osborne ✝ **1996**

Postmodernism, a disputed term that has occupied much recent debate about contemporary culture since the early 1980s. In its simplest and least satisfactory sense it refers generally to the phase of 20th-century Western culture that succeeded the reign of high modernism, thus indicating the products of the 'space age' after some time in the 1950s. More often, though, it is applied to a cultural condition prevailing in the advanced capitalist societies since the 1960s, characterized by a superabundance of disconnected images and styles - most noticeably in television, advertising, commercial design, and pop video. In this sense, promoted by Jean Baudrillard and other commentators, post-modernity is said to be a culture of fragmentary sensations, eclectic nostalgia, disposable simulacra, and promiscuous superficiality, in which the traditionally valued qualities of depth, coherence, meaning, originality, and authenticity are evacuated or dissolved amid the random swirl of empty signals.

As applied to literature and other arts, the term is notoriously ambiguous, implying either that modernism has been superseded or that it has continued into a new phase. Postmodernism may be seen as a continuation of modernism's alienated mood and disorienting techniques and at the same time as an abandonment of its determined quest for artistic coherence in a fragmented world: in very crude terms, where a modernist artist or writer would try to wrest a meaning from the world through myth, symbol, or formal complexity, the postmodernist greets the absurd or meaningless confusion of contemporary existence with a certain numbed or flippant indifference, favouring self-consciously 'depthless' works of fabulation, pastiche, bricolage, or aleatory disconnection. The term cannot usefully serve as an inclusive description of all literature since the 1950s or 1960s, but is applied selectively to those works that display most evidently the moods and formal disconnections described above. It seems to have no relevance to modern poetry, and little to drama, but is used widely in reference to fiction, notably to the novels and stories of Thomas Pynchon, Kurt Vonnegut, Italo Calvino, Vladimir Nabkokov, William S. Burroughs, and Angela Carter. Some of their works, like Pynchon's *Gravity's Rainbow* (1973) and Nabokov's *Ada* (1969), employ devices reminiscent of science fiction, playing with contradictory orders of reality or the irruption of the fabulous into the secular world.

Opinion is still divided, however, on the value of the term and of the phenomenon it purports to describe. Those who most often use it tend to welcome 'the postmodern' as a liberation from the hierarchy of 'high' and 'low' cultures; while sceptics (sometimes dismissively referring to the postmodern enthusiasts as 'posties') regard the term as a symptom of irresponsible academic euphoria about the glitter of consumerist capitalism and its moral vacuity. For more extended discussions, consult Jean-François Lyotard, The Postmodern Condition (1986); H.Bertens and D.Fokkema(eds.), Approaching Postmodernism (1986); and Brian McHale, Postmodernist Fiction (1987).

    1981 S.Plath, Collected Poems   **1990** A.Byatt, Possession
      1982 T.Hughes, *Selected Poems* **1957-1981**   **1991** J.Richardson, *A Life of Picasso*
           1992 B.Unsworth, *Sacred Hunger*
       1988 *Graham Swift Waterland*
    1983 M.Bradbury, *Rates of Exchange*
      1986 W.Golding, *The Paperman*
      1986 K.Amis, *The old Devil*
      1987 P.Lively, *Moon Tiger*

1980 H.Brenton, *The Romans in Britain*
Edward Bond
1980 *The Worlds*   **1988** H.Pinter, *Mountain Language*
   1981 *Restoration*   **1985** P.Schaffer, *Yonadab*
    1982 *Summer*

1980 1981 1982 1983 1984 1985 1986 1987 1988 1989 1990 1991 1992 1993 1994 1995 1996 1997 1998 1999 2000

2000 2001 2002 2003 2004 2005 2006 2007 2008 2009 2010 2011 2012 2013 2014 2015 2016 2017 2018 2019 2020

2000 George Bush winner of US presidential election. Theresa May resigns as Prime Minister June 7, **2019**

2002 6.2. Queen Elizabeth celebrates her Golden Jubilee Boris Johnson succeeds Theresa May July 26 **2019**

2002 9.6.Funeral of Queen Elizabeth The Queen Mother at –Westminster Abbey

2003 March 20 – The Iraq War begins with the invasions of Iraq by the US and allied forces

2003 September 6 - Europe's busiest shopping centre, the Bull Ring in Birmingham, is officially opened

2003 October 26 - Concorde makes its last commercial flight, bringing the era of airliner supersonic travel to an end

2006 January 8 – The RMS Queen Mary 2, at the time the largest ocean liner ever built, is christened by its namesake's granddaughter, Queen Elizabeth II.

2006 May 1 – The European Union expands by 10 new member states:
Cyprus, the Czech Republic, Estonia, Hungary,Latvia, Lithuania, Malta, Poland, Slovakia, and Slovenia

2006 November 2 – George W. Bush is re-elected President of the United States.

2005 March 26 - The first episode of the revived series of *Doctor Who* airs on BBC One.

2005 April 9 – Charles, Prince of Wales marries Camilla Parker Bowles in a civil ceremony at Windsor's
Camilla receives the title Duchess of Cornwall   Guildhall.

2005 May 25 - Liverpool win the UEFA Champions League after a penalty shootout against AC Milan.

2005 July 7 – Four coordinated suicide bombings hit central London, killing 52 people and injuring over 700.

2006 December 29 – UK settles its Anglo-American loan, post-WWII loan debt.

2007 January 1 - Bulgaria and Romania join the European Union, while Slovenia joins the
Eurozone.   passengers.

2007 November 16 – High Speed 1 from London to the Channel Tunnel is opened to

2007 December 21 At the age of 81 years, 266 days, Queen Elizabeth II became the oldest ever reigning British monarch, surpassing Queen Victoria who was aged 81 years, 263 days upon her death on January 22, 1901.

2007 The Czech Republic, Estonia, Hungary, Latvia, Lithuania, Malta, Poland, Slovakia, and Slovenia join the Schengen border-free zone

2008 January 1 – Cyprus and Malta adopt the euro

2008 October 3 – Global financial crisis: U.S. President George W. Bush signs the Revised Emergency Economic Stabilization Act into law, creating a 700 billion Dollar Treasury fund to purchase failing bank assets

2008 November 6 – Democratic U.S. Senator Barack Obama is elected the 66th President of the United States, making him the first African-American president.

2008 December 10 – The Channel Island of Sark, a British Crown dependency, holds its first fully democratic elections under a new constitutional arrangement, becoming the last European territory to abolish feudalism

2009 June 11 – The outbreak of the H1N1 influenza strain, commonly re ferred to as "swine flu", is deemed a global pandemic.

2011 April 29 – An estimated two billion people watch the wedding of Prince William, Duke of Cambridge and Catherine Middleton at West minster Abbey in London.

2012 February 6 – The Diamond Jubilee of Queen Eliza beth II marks the 60th anniversary of her accession to the thrones of the United Kingdom, Canada, Australia, and New Zealand, and the 60th anniversary of her becoming Head of the Commonwealth

After 266 years since its first publication, the *Encyclopædia* **2012** March 13 - *Britannica* discontinues its print edition

The 2012 Summer Olympics are held in London, England, United Kingdom **2012** July 27 – August 12

Barack Obama is re-elected President of the United States **2012** November 6

UK General Election results in the first Conservative majority government in 18 years **2015** May 7 – .

The United Kingdom votes in a referendum to leave the European Union **2016** June 23 –

The Maldives announces its decision to withdraw from the Commonwealth of Nations. **2016** October 13 –

2016 November 8 –
Businessman and television personality Donald Trump is elected the 65th President of the United States in a surprise victory against his opponent, former Secretary of State Hillary Clinton

A terrorist attack outside the Palace of Westminster in London, England, kills five people and injures **2017** March 22 –
more than fifty others.

The United Kingdom triggers Article 50 of the Lisbon Treaty, starting the Brexit negotiations, **2017** March 29 –
the talks for the United Kingdom to leave the European Union.

London Bridge attack: Eight people are murdered and dozens of civilians are wounded by Islamist terrorists. **2017** June 3 –
Three of the attackers are shot dead by the police.

In the midst of Brexit, a snap general election is held in the UK, three years before the next is due, resulting **2017** June 8 –
in a hung parliament, with the Conservative Party, led by Prime Minister Theresa May, losing their majority in Parliament. The Labour Party, led by Jeremy Corbyn, makes gains for the first time since 1997. Days later, the Conservative Party, now lacking a majority, enters a confidence-and-supply deal with the Northern Irish DUP

A fire at Grenfell Tower in London, England, kills 72 people and injures more than 70 others **2017** June 16 –

The 2018 Commonwealth Games are held in Gold Coast, Queensland, Australia. 6 – 15 April **2018**

The wedding of Prince Harry and Meghan Markle was held at St George's Chapel, England, May 19 – **2018**
with an estimated global audience of 1.9 billion

Gatwick Airport drone incident: Reports of drone sightings close to the runway at 19–21 December **2018**
Gatwick Airport in England causes major disruption, affecting approximately 160,000 passengers and 1,000 flights, making it the largest disruption since ash from an Icelandic volcano shut the airport in 2010 –

WikiLeaks co-founder Julian Assange is arrested after seven years in Ecuador's embassy in London April 11 **2019**

British Prime Minister Theresa May announces her resignation as Conservative leader, effective June 7, **2019**.

2000 2001 2002 2003 2004 2005 2006 2007 2008 2009 2010 2011 2012 2013 2014 2015 2016 2017 2018 2019 2020

The Supreme Court of the United Kingdom unanimously rules in R (Miller) v The Prime Minister that the September 2019 prorogation of Parliament is unlawful and void — September 26 **2019**

COVID-19 pandemic: First known human case of Coronavirus disease 2019, in Wuhan, Hubei, China December 1 **2019**

The United Kingdom and Gibraltar formally withdraw from the European Union, beginning an 11-month transition period January 31 **2020**

COVID-19 pandemic: The U.K. death toll from COVID-19 becomes the highest in Europe at 32,313 after exceeding May 5 **2020**

A 1636 edition of *The Two Noble Kinsmen*, the last play by English playwright William Shakespeare, is discovered September 19 **2020** at the Royal Scots College's library in Salamanca, Spain. It is believed to be the oldest copy of any of his works in the country

The EU began legal proceedings against the UK after it ignored their deadline to drop controversial sections October 1 **2020** from its internal market Bill

At the end of an 11-year demining process, the Falkland Islands are declared free of land mines, 38 years after October 23 **2020** the end of the 1982 war

2020 United States presidential election: Joe Biden is elected as the 66th President of the United States November 7 **2020** after remaining vote counts (November 7) come in from key states delayed by an influx of mail-in ballots caused by the pandemic, defeating the incumbent President Donald Trump

COVID-19 pandemic: The United Kingdom becomes the first nation to begin a mass inoculation campaign using a December 8 **2020** clinically authorised, fully tested vaccine, Pfizer–BioNTech COVID-19 vaccine

The United Kingdom and the European Union agree to a comprehensive free trade agreement prior to the December 26 **2020** end of the transition period

The transition period following the United Kingdom's exit from the European Union on 31 January 2020 expires. December 31 **2020**

"the Gherkin", completed in 2003 at 180 metres tall   Canary Wharf   The Shard, completed in 2012 at 309.6 metres tall

2003 January 3 ✳ Greta Thunberg, Swedish climate activist
2003 November 8 ✳ Lady Louise Windsor, British royalty
2007 December 17 ✳ James, Viscount Severn, grandson of Elizabeth II, son of The Earl and Countess of Wessex

Prince George of Cambridge ✳ **2013** July 22 –
Princess Charlotte of Cambridge ✳ **2015** May 2 –
Prince Louis of Cambridge, fifth in line to the throne of the United Kingdom ✳ April 23 **2018**

2003 June 26 ✞ Denis Thatcher, British businessman and husband of Margaret Thatcher (b. 1915)
2003 July 25 ✞ John Schlesinger, English film director (b. 1926)   1911)
2006 June 5 ✞ Ronald Reagan, American politician and actor, 60th President of the United States (b.
2006 October 29 ✞ Princess Alice, Duchess of Gloucester (b. 1901)
2005 July 17 ✞ Edward Heath, 68th Prime Minister of the United Kingdom (b. 1916)
2005 November 5 ✞ John Fowles, English novelist (b. 1926)
2006 March 9 ✞ John Profumo, British politician (b. 1915)
Margaret Hilda Thatcher, Baroness Thatcher, LG, OM, DStJ, PC, FRS, HonFRSC née Roberts; ✳13 October 1925. ✞8 April **2013**
Terry Pratchett, English writer (b. 1968) ✞ **2015** March 12
Stephen Hawking, English theoretical physicist and cosmologist (b. 1962) ✞ March 16 **2018**
Andrea Levy, English novelist (b. 1956) ✞ February 16 **2019**
John le Carré, English author (b. 1931) ✞ December 12 **2020**